Only & Only NCERT
The Best Way to Practice NCERT...

NCERT
MCQs

Indian Economy

Class 9-12 *(Old+New)*

Highly Useful for UPSC, State PSCs
and Other Competitive Exams

NCERT MCQs

Indian Economy

Class 9-12 *(Old+New)*

Author
Rakesh Kumar Roshan

ARIHANT PUBLICATIONS (INDIA) LIMITED

ॐ © **Publisher**

ॐ **Administrative & Production Offices**

Regd. Office

'Ramchhaya' 4577/15, Agarwal Road, Darya Ganj, New Delhi -110002
Tele: 011- 47630600, 43518550

ॐ **Head Office**

Kalindi, TP Nagar, Meerut (UP) - 250002,
Tel: 0121-7156203, 7156204

ॐ **Sales & Support Offices**

Agra, Ahmedabad, Bengaluru, Bareilly, Chennai, Delhi, Guwahati, Hyderabad, Jaipur, Jhansi, Kolkata, Lucknow, Nagpur & Pune.

PO No : TXT-XX-XXXXXXX-X-XX

Published by Arihant Publications (India) Ltd.

For further information about the books published by Arihant, log on to www.arihantbooks.com or e-mail at info@arihantbooks.com

Follow us on   

Your Achievement
Our Commitment

BEFORE ANYTHING ELSE, PREPARATION IS THE KEY TO SUCCESS.

Civil Services Examinations are the most prestigious and coveted examinations in India. Due to the power, authority, reputation, this career attracts every aspirant to hold the post and become IAS/IPS officer. Union Public Service Commission (UPSC) and State Public Service Commission (SPSC) conduct this examination every year and lakhs of aspirants across the country toil for years to crack this distinguished exam in the country.

Being the toughest exam, it automatically consists of a vast and a detailed syllabus. Aspirants often find it difficult to cover the entire syllabus and lack a right direction for a proper and a systematic study for the exam.

The most important aspect of this preparation journey is the NCERT books. Every year approximately 35-40 questions directly come from NCERT books.

NCERT books also play a key role in understanding the Basic Concepts; so that aspirants can easily form the basic foundation of the entire syllabus. But due to the demand for many NCERT books which are required for study, it becomes exhausting to cover each and every NCERT book.

NCERT MCQs series presented by Arihant Publications covers MCQS from Class 9th to 12th NCERT books (both Old & New) in a comprehensive manner. The series is extremely useful for UPSC and State PSC examinations. The chapter-wise questions given in the sequential form in the series along with the source of the questions and detailed solutions will make the preparation easy and convenient. The factual accuracy and explanations make this series an authentic source for cracking the examinations.

The book is adorned with questions prepared by a team of experts along with a vital role played by the Project Management team with members: Mona Yadav (Project Manager), Divya Gusain (Project Coordinator), Shivani Dixit, Ayush Rajput, Chandan (Proof readers), Vinay Sharma, Kamal Kishor, Sonu Kumar (DTP coordinators), Shanu and Mazher (Cover and Inner designer).

We hope this book will help the aspirants to achieve their goals of clearing UPSC as well as State PCS exams. Your valuable suggestions have always inspired us to strive for useful, authentic and more trustworthy publications. So your inputs and suggestions are welcomed for subsequent editions.

We wish you all the very best for your preparation and journey!!

Publisher

CONTENTS

01

Economy : An Introduction

New NCERT Class IX (The Story of Village Palampur), New NCERT Class IX (People as a Resource), Old NCERT Class IX & X (An Overview of the Indian Economy), New NCERT Class X (Sectors of the Indian Economy), New NCERT Class X (Development), New NCERT Class XI (Indian Economy 1950-1990), New NCERT Class XI (Indian Economy on the Eve of Independence), New NCERT Class XI (Human Capital Formation in India), New NCERT Class XI (Environment and Sustainable Development), New NCERT Class XII (Introduction)

1. Who is regarded as 'Father of Modern Economics'?　　*(Chap 1, Class-XII, New NCERT)*

(MPPSC Pre 2010)

(a) Adam Smith　　(b) Marshal

(c) Keynes　　(d) Robins

↗ *Ans.* *(a)*

Exp. Adam Smith is regarded as 'Father of Modern Economics'. His work published in 1766 'An Enquiry into the Nature and Causes of the Wealth of Nations' is regarded as the first major comprehensive book on the subject. It is a fundamental work in classical economics, which deals with topics of division of labour, productivity and free markets.

2. With regard to the difference between micro and macro economics, which of the following statement(s) is/are correct?

(Chap 1, Class-XII, New NCERT)

1. In macroeconomics, aggregate output of goods and services at the level of nation is measured whereas in microeconomics, individual factors of production are studied.
2. Macroeconomic policies are pursued by the state itself or statutory bodies like the Reserve Bank of India (RBI) whereas policies concerning microeconomics are pursued by individual agents only.

Codes

(a) Only 1　　(b) Only 2

(c) Both 1 and 2　　(d) Neither 1 nor 2

↗ *Ans.* *(a)*

Exp. Statement (1) is correct with regard to the difference between micro and macro economics as in macroeconomics, the aggregate output of goods and services, employment level, price level, etc are measured at the level of nation whereas microeconomics focuses on issues that affect individuals and companies.

However, both are interrelated and interdependent as macroeconomics takes into account various interlinkages, which may exist between different sectors of the economy.

Statement (2) is incorrect as other than economic decision taken by individual agents (such as household or automobile company), the action of entire sector such as automobile industry are also studied in microeconomics. It is also governed by state and the regulatory bodies like RBI.

3. Which of the given pairs of personality and associated field is not correctly matched?

(Chap 1, Class-XII, New NCERT)

(a)　Adam Smith　　– Modern Economics

(b)　John Maynard Keynes　　– Macroeconomics

(c)　Physiocrats of France　　– Social Economics

(d)　All of the above

➤ *Ans.* (c)

Exp. Among the given pairs, pair (c) is not correctly matched. Physiocrats of France were prominent thinkers of Political Economics (not Social Economics) before Adam Smith. They studied action of the state and its impact on different economic variables.

4. Mixed economy means an economy where

(Chap 2, Class-XII-New NCERT)

(a) both agriculture and industry are equally promoted by the state.

(b) there is co-existence of public sector along with private sector.

(c) there is importance of small scale industries along with heavy industries.

(d) economy is controlled by military as well as civilian rulers.

➤ *Ans.* (b)

Exp. Mixed economy means an economy where there is co-existence of public sector along with private sector.

A mixed economy is an economic system that combines elements of a capitalist, market based system, with a socialist, command economy system. It mixes elements such as private property rights, free trade, and privatisation, with socialist element such as regulation, the welfare state and re-distribution.

5. With reference to the types of economies, which of the following statements is incorrect?

(Chap 1, Class-XII, New NCERT)

(a) In a centrally planned economy, the government or the central authority plans all the important activities in the economy.

(b) In a market economy, the central problems regarding how much and what to produce are solved through the coordination of economic activities brought about by the price signal.

(c) In a mixed economy, society has no private property since everything is owned by the state.

(d) In capitalist economy, purchasing power determines production and distribution of goods.

➤ *Ans.* (c)

Exp. Statement (c) is incorrect with reference to the types of economies.

In a mixed economy, all the important decisions regarding production, distribution and consumption of goods and services are taken jointly by the government and the private sector.

The right of private property is protected under mixed economy and the complete state ownership of all the resources is a characteristic of the communist economy.

6. Consider the following characteristics of an economy.

(Chap 1, Class-XII, New NCERT)

1. There is private ownership of means of production.

2. Production takes place for selling the output in the market.

3. There is sale and purchase of labour services at a price, which is called the wage rate.

Which of the following types of economies is represented by the above characteristics?

(a) Capitalist Economy   (b) Socialist Economy

(c) Mixed Economy   (d) All of these

➤ *Ans.* (a)

Exp. The given characteristics represents the capitalist economy. Capitalist economy is a type of economy that is represented by given characteristics.

In a capitalist economy, there is private ownership of means of production and the means of production are driven by the motive of profit-making. Production takes place for selling the output in the market.

In such economy, there is sale and purchase of labour services at a price which is called the wage rate (the labour that is sold and purchased against wages is referred to as 'wage labour'). Other characteristics of capitalist economy is minimal or no intervention of state, free market and Laissez Faire.

7. The working of the price mechanism in a free-market economy refers to which one of the following?

(Chap 2, Class-XII, New NCERT)

(a) The interplay of the forces of demand and supply.

(b) Determination of the inflation rate in the economy.

(c) Determination of the economy's propensity to consume.

(d) Determination of the economy's full employment output.

➤ *Ans.* (a)

Exp. The working of the price mechanism in a free-market economy refers to the interplay of the forces of demand and supply. In the market economy (or capitalist economy) only those consumer goods are produced that are in demand. Purchasing power is the main determinant of production, consumption and distribution of goods in a free-market economy.

8. A closed economy is an economy, in which

(Chap I, Class XII, New NCERT) (IAS Pre 2010)

(a) the money supply is fully controlled.

(b) deficit financing takes place.

(c) only export takes place.

(d) neither export nor import takes place.

↗ Ans. *(d)*

Exp. Closed economy is an economy in which neither export nor import takes place as no activity is conducted with other economies. It is self-sufficient, where no imports are brought in and no exports are sent out. The goal is to provide consumers with everything that they need from within the economy.

9. Manufacturing does not include, which of the following?

(Chap 2, Class IX & X, Old NCERT) (CGPSC Pre 2017)

(a) Large industries   (b) Medium industries
(c) Small industries   (d) Real estate industries

↗ Ans. *(d)*

Exp. Manufacturing (or industrial sector) does not include Real estate industries. It includes those activities in which natural products are changed into finished goods, through means of manufacturing.

The small, medium and large scale industries, which are involved in producing manufactured goods such as steel, textiles, automobiles etc are included in secondary sector. Real estate industries are generally included as a part of tertiary (or service) sector.

10. Which of the following is the correct increasing order of the contribution of the three sectors to the GDP of India? *(Chap 2, Class-X, New NCERT)*

(a) Agriculture < Service < Industry
(b) Agriculture < Industry < Service
(c) Service < Industry < Agriculture
(d) Industry < Agriculture < Service

↗ Ans. *(b)*

Exp. The correct increasing order of the contribution of the three sectors to the GDP of India is Agriculture < Industry < Service.

Gross Domestic Product (GDP) is the value of all final goods and services produced within a country during a particular year. According to RBI's, 2021 estimates the contribution of agriculture, industry and service sector in Indian GDP is 20.19%, 25.92% and 53.89% respectively.

11. Public and private sectors are differentiated on the basis of which of the following?

(Chap 2, Class-X, New NCERT)

(a) Conditions of employment
(b) Nature of economic activity
(c) Ownership of the enterprises
(d) None of the above

↗ Ans. *(c)*

Exp. Public and private sectors are differentiated on the basis of 'ownership of the enterprises'. In private sector, ownership of assets and delivery of services is in the hands of private individuals or companies.

They are guided by the motive to earn profits. In case of public sector, public service and establishment of essential infrastructure are the guiding principles. In public sector, government owns the assets and is responsible for delivery of services.

12. Consider the following statements.

(Chap 2, Class-X, New NCERT)

1. Primary sector is called so because it forms the base for all other products that we subsequently make.
2. Since, most of the natural products we get are from agriculture, dairy, fishing, forestry, this sector is also called agriculture and related sectors.

Which of the statement(s) given above is/are correct?

(a) Only 1   (b) Only 2
(c) Both 1 and 2   (d) Neither 1 nor 2

↗ Ans. *(c)*

Exp. Both the statements (1) and (2) are correct. When we produce a good by exploiting natural resources, it is an activity of primary sector. It forms the base for all other products. Since, most of the natural products we get are from agriculture, dairy, fishing and forestry, this sector is called agriculture and related sector. For example, cotton, milk production, minerals and ores.

13. Consider the following statements.

(Chap 2, Class-X, New NCERT)

1. Tertiary activities, by themselves, do not produce a good but they are an aid or a support for the production process.
2. Transport, banking, storage, communication and trade are some examples of tertiary activities.

Which of the statement(s) given above is/are correct?

(a) Only 1   (b) Only 2
(c) Both 1 and 2   (d) Neither 1 nor 2

↗ Ans. *(c)*

Exp. Both the statements (1) and (2) are correct. Tertiary sector helps in the development of primary and secondary sectors. These activities, by themselves do not produce a good but they are an aid and support for the production process. Since, these activities generate services rather than goods, the tertiary sector is also called the service sector.

For example, goods that are produced in the primary or secondary sector would need to be transported by trucks or trains and then sold in wholesale and retail shops.

Transport, banking, storage, communication and trade are some examples of tertiary activities.

14. Consider the following statements.

(Chap 2, Class-XI, New NCERT)

1. Usually with economic development, the share of agriculture to the GDP declines and the share of the service sector becomes dominant.
2. At higher levels of development, the industrial sector contributes more to the GDP than the service sector.

Which of the statement(s) given above is/are correct?

(a) Only 1   (b) Only 2
(c) Both 1 and 2   (d) Neither 1 nor 2

↗ *Ans.* *(d)*

Exp. Neither statement (1) nor (2) is correct.

The economic development of the country is usually characterised by structural changes in the economy. At the first stage of development, the share of agriculture declines whereas share of industrial sector (not service sector) becomes dominant.

At higher levels of development, the service sector contributes more to the GDP than the other two sectors. India is considered as exception to this traditional model of economic growth as the share of agriculture in GDP (which was 50% in early 1950s) declined and was overshadowed by the service sector, which became most important sector of the Indian economy.

15. Consider the following statements regarding economic growth.   *(Chap 2, Class-XI, New NCERT)*

1. It refers to an increase in the country's capacity to produce the output of goods and services in an economy.
2. It implies either a larger stock of productive capital, or a larger size of supporting services like transport and banking, or an increase in the efficiency of productive capital and services.

Which of the statement(s) given above is/are correct?

(a) Only 1   (b) Only 2
(c) Both 1 and 2   (d) Neither 1 nor 2

↗ *Ans.* *(c)*

Exp. Both the statements (1) and (2) are correct regarding economic growth.

Economic growth is the increase in the value of an economy's goods and services. It is an increase in the capacity of an economy to produce goods and services.

A steady increase in Gross Domestic Product (GDP) is considered as good indicator of growth. It is considered as quantitative assessment of economic growth and is measured as increased stock of productive capital or services.

16. Which of the following statements is correct regarding development? *(Chap 1, Class-X, New NCERT)*

1. Different persons could have different as well as conflicting notions of a country's development.
2. Different persons can have different developmental goals.
3. Development for one, may even be destructive for the other.

Codes
(a) Only 1   (b) 1 and 2
(c) 2 and 3   (d) 1, 2 and 3

↗ *Ans.* *(d)*

Exp. All the statements (1), (2) and (3) are correct regarding development.

Different people have different developmental goals. For example, for landless labours, more days of work and better wages are the developmental goals.

On the other hand, for prosperous farmers from Punjab, high family income through higher support price for their crops will be the developmental goal.

17. Consider the following statements with reference to human capital.   *(Chap 5, Class-XI, New NCERT)*

1. We need good human capital to produce other human capital.
2. Investment in education is considered as one of the main sources of human capital.

Which of the statement(s) given above is/are correct?

(a) Only 1   (b) Only 2
(c) Both 1 and 2   (d) Neither 1 nor 2

↗ *Ans.* *(c)*

Exp. Both the statements (1) and (2) are correct regarding the human capital.

We need good human capital to produce other human capital, which means we need investment in human development to produce more human capital out of human resources.

Investment in education is considered as one of the main sources of human capital as spending on education by individuals is similar to spending on capital goods by companies with the objective of increasing future profits over a long period of time.

18. Who among the following has given the concept of human development?

(Chap 3, Class XII, New NCERT)

(a) Amartya Sen   (b) Mahbub-ul-Haq
(c) Sukhamoy Chakravarty   (c) GS Chanda

↗ *Ans.* *(b)*

Exp. The concept of human development was given by Pakistani economist, Mahbub-ul-Haq. It is defined as a process of enlarging the range of people's choices and increasing their opportunities for education, health care, income and empowerment.

19. Which of the following are considered to be the four pillars of human development?

(Chap 3, Class-XII, New NCERT)

(a) Equity, inclusion, productivity and empowerment.

(b) Equity, productivity, empowerment and sustainability.

(c) Productivity, gender, inclusion and equity.

(d) Labour, productivity, inclusion and equity.

↗ *Ans. (b)*

Exp. Equity, productivity, empowerment and sustainability are considered to be the four pillars of human development. Equity refers to making equal access to opportunities available to everybody.

Productivity means enrichment of human capital and empowerment refers to power to make choices. Sustainability means continuity in the availability of opportunities.

20. Which of the following statements is incorrect regarding the difference between physical capital and human capital? *(Chap 5, Class-XI, New NCERT)*

(a) Physical capital is intangible and human capital is tangible.

(b) Physical capital can be easily sold in the market whereas human capital is not sold in the market.

(c) The physical capital is separable from its owner, whereas, human capital is inseparable from its owner.

(d) None of the above

↗ *Ans. (a)*

Exp. Statement (a) is incorrect regarding the difference between physical capital and human capital as physical capital is tangible and can be easily sold in the market like any other commodity on the other hand, human capital is intangible and is not sold in the market. Only the services of the human capital are sold.

21. Which of the following committees is related to the scheme for development of human capital?

(a) Santhanam Committee *(Chap 5, Class-XI, New NCERT)*

(b) Tarapore Committee

(c) Tapas Majumdar Committee

(d) Bimal Jalan Committee

↗ *Ans. (c)*

Exp. Tapas Majumdar Committee is related to the scheme for development of human capital.

The Tapas Majumdar Committee was appointed in 1999 to look into the inadequacy of the expenditure on education, which is the source of human capital. He estimated an expenditure of around ₹ 1.37 lakh crore over 10 years (1998-99 to 2006-07) to bring all children in the age group of 6-14 years under the purview of school education. This committee recommended the desired level of education expenditure of around 6% of GDP.

22. Consider the following statements.

(Chap 5, Class-XI, New NCERT)

1. Physical capital is completely mobile between countries except for some artificial trade restrictions.

2. Human capital is not perfectly mobile between countries as movement is restricted by nationality and culture.

Which of the statement(s) given above is/are correct?

(a) Only 1 (b) Only 2

(c) Both 1 and 2 (d) Neither 1 nor 2

↗ *Ans. (c)*

Exp. Both the statements (1) and (2) are correct. Physical capital formation can be built even through imports whereas human capital formation is to be done through conscious policy formulations in consonance with the nature of the society and economy and expenditure by the state and the individuals.

23. Which of the following organisations publishes the Human Development Report?

(a) IMF *(Chap 1, Class-X, New NCERT)*

(b) World Bank

(c) UNDP

(d) World Economic Forum

↗ *Ans. (c)*

Exp. United Nations Development Programme (UNDP) publishes the Human Development Report.

It compares countries based on the educational levels of the people, their health status and per capita income. In other words, it is a statistic composite index of life expectancy, education (mean years of schooling completed and expected years of schooling upon entering the school) and Per Capita Income.

24. Which of the following parameters is not included in the Human Development Index?

(Chap 1, Class-X, New NCERT) (UPPSC Pre 2020)

(a) Per Capita Income (b) Life expectancy at birth

(c) Social inequality (d) Education

↗ *Ans. (c)*

Exp. Social inequality is not included in the Human Development Index. Human Development Index is released by United Nations Development Programme (UNDP). It includes the following parameters :
- Life expectancy at birth
- Education (Mean years of schooling and expected years of schooling)
- Per Capita Income

25. Which of the following statements is correct about human development? *(Chap 2, Class-IX, New NCERT)*

(a) The expenditure on education has constantly increased over the last 5 years.
(b) The expenditure on health has constantly decreased over the last 5 years.
(c) Literacy among males is nearly 14.4% higher than females and it is about 16% higher in urban areas as compared to rural areas.
(d) All of the above

↗ *Ans.* *(c)*

Exp. Statement (c) is correct about human development. As per Census 2011, the literacy rate at all India level is 72.98% and the literacy rate for females and males are 64.63% and 80.9% respectively. Thus, literacy among males is nearly 14.4% higher than females.

In the rural areas, the literacy rate is 68.91% and in urban, it is 84.98%, hence, literacy rate is about 16% higher in urban areas as compared to rural areas.

Statements (a) and (b) are incorrect as illustrated by the table given below

Year	Expenditure	
	Health	Education
2021-22 (estimated)	₹ 2,23,846 crore	₹ 93,224 crore
2020-21	₹ 67,112 crore	₹ 99,300 crore
2019-20	₹ 61,398 crore	₹ 94,854 crore
2018-19	₹ 54,600 crore	₹ 85,010 crore
2017-18	₹ 48,853 crore	₹ 79,685 crore

Hence, the expenditure on education has fluctuated over the last five years whereas the expenditure on health has increased over the span of last five years.

26. Consider the following Assertion(A) and Reason (R) and choose the correct code.

(Chap 5, Class-XI, New NCERT)

Assertion (A) Human development is based on the idea that education and health are integral to human well-being.

Reason (R) Only when people have the ability to read and write and the ability to lead a long and healthy life, they will be able to make other choices, which they value.

Codes
(a) Both A and R are true and R is the correct explanation of A.
(b) Both A and R are true, but R is not the correct explanation of A.
(c) A is true, but R is false.
(d) A is false, but R is true.

↗ *Ans.* *(a)*

Exp. Both Assertion (A) and Reason (R) are true and Reason (R) is the correct explanation of Assertion (A). Human development is based on the idea that education and health are integral to human well-being. It is because only when the people have the ability to read and write alongwith the ability to lead a long and healthy life, they will be able to make other choices which they value. In such a view, every individual has the right to get basic education and basic healthcare i.e., every individual has the right to be literate and lead a healthy life.

27. Saving energy and other resources for the future without sacrificing people's comfort in the present is the definition of, which of the following concepts?

(Chap 9, Class XII, New NCERT) (UPPSC Pre 2018)

(a) Economic Growth
(b) Economic Development
(c) Sustainable Development
(d) Human Development

↗ *Ans.* *(c)*

Exp. Saving energy and other resources for the future without sacrificing people's comfort in the present is defined as sustainable development. The concept of sustainable development was emphasised by the United Nations Conference on Environment and Development (UNCED), which defined it as, 'development that meets the needs of present generation without compromising, the ability of future generation to meet their own needs'.

28. Consider the following statements.

(Chap 9, Class-XI, New NCERT)

1. India supports approximately 17% of the world's human and 20% of livestock population on a mere 2.5% of the world's geographical area.
2. The CPCB (Central Pollution Control Board) has identified seventeen categories of industries (large and medium scale) as significantly polluting.

Which of the statement(s) given above is/are correct?

(a) Only 1
(b) Only 2
(c) Both 1 and 2
(d) Neither 1 nor 2

↗ *Ans.* (c)

Exp. Both the statements (1) and (2) are correct.

India supports approximately 17% of the world's human and 20% of livestock population on a mere 2.5% of the world's geographical area. The high density of population and livestock and the competing use of land for forestry, agriculture, etc. exert enormous pressure on the country's resources.

The CPCB (Central Pollution Control Board) has identified seventeen categories of industries (large and medium scale) as significantly polluting. The CPCB was established in 1974. This board prepares manuals, codes and guidelines relatives to treatment and disposal of sewage and trade effluents.

29. **Which of the following is not one of the strategies for sustainable development?**

   (Chap 9, Class-XI, New NCERT)

   (a) Use of conventional sources of energy
   (b) Use of LPG and gobar gas in rural areas
   (c) Use of CNG in urban areas
   (d) Use of solar power through photovoltaic cells

   ↗ *Ans.* (a)

   Exp. Use of conventional sources of energy is not the strategy for sustainable development.

   Use of non-conventional sources of energy (solar power, wind power, etc), LPG (Liquefied Petroleum Gas), gobar gas in rural areas, CNG (Compressed Natural Gas) in urban areas, and solar power through photovoltaic cells are some of the strategies for sustainable development.

   These methods are not only sustainable but they are also environment-friendly. These practices reduce deforestation and pollution.

30. **Consider the following Assertion(A) and Reason (R) and choose the correct code.**

   (Chap 9, Class-XI, New NCERT)

   Assertion (A) Development that ignores its repercussions on the environment will destroy the environment that sustains life forms.

   Reason (R) Environment and economy are interdependent and need each other.

Codes

(a) Both A and R are true and R is the correct explanation of A.
(b) Both A and R are true, but R is not the correct explanation of A.
(c) A is true, but R is false.
(d) A is false, but R is true.

↗ *Ans.* (a)

Exp. Both Assertion (A) and Reason (R) are true and Reason (R) is the correct explanation of Assertion (A).

Development that ignores its repercussions on the environment will destroy the environment that sustains life forms.

Environment and economy are interdependent and need each other. For that, they need sustainable development, which is a development that will allow all future generations to have a potential average quality of life.

31. **Which one of the following is not a Sustainable Development Goal adopted by United Nations?**

   (Chap 9, Class XI, New NCERT)

   (a) Quality education
   (b) No poverty
   (c) Clean water and sanitation
   (d) Child mortality

   ↗ *Ans.* (d)

   Exp. Only child mortality is not consider under new 17 Sustainable Development goals. The United Nations General Assembly (UNGA) formally adopted the 2030 Agenda for sustainable development on 26th September, 2015. New framework of 17 goals and 169 targets adopted by 193 members of UNGA.

   17 SDGs are – no poverty, zero hunger, good health and well-being, quality education, gender equality, clean water and sanitation, affordable and clean energy, decent work and economic growth, industry, innovation and infrastructure, reduced inequality sustainable cities and communities, responsible consumption and production, climate action, life below water, life on land, peace, justice and strong institution and partnership for the goals.

02
National Income and Accounting

New NCERT Class X (Sectors of the Indian Economy), **New NCERT Class X** (Development),
New NCERT Class XI (Indian Economy on the Eve of Independence), **Old NCERT Class XI** (Composition
of Macroeconomy and Accounting of Natural Income), **New NCERT Class XII** (Accounting of National Income),
Old NCERT Class XII (Accounting of National Income : Concepts and Measurement)

1. Who among the following introduced the use of national income aggregates to assess the direction of growth of economies?

(Chap 3, Class-XII, Old NCERT)

(a) JM Keynes (b) Richard Stone
(c) Simon Kuznets (d) Adam Smith

➤ *Ans.* (c)

Exp. Simon Kuznets introduced the use of national income aggregates to assess the direction of growth of economies. He defined national income as "the net output of commodities and services flowing during the year from the country's productive system in the hands of the ultimate consumers."

According to Kuznets, national income can be calculated by following three methods
(i) Product method (ii) Income method
(iii) Consumption method

2. Whose estimate about India's national and Per Capita Income during the colonial period was considered most significant?

(Chap 1, Class-XI, New NCERT)

(a) RC Dutta (b) Dadabhai Naoroji
(c) RC Desai (d) VKRV Rao

➤ *Ans.* (d)

Exp. VKRV Rao's estimate about India's national and Per Capita Income during the colonial period was considered most significant. The first scientific method to estimate India's national and Per Capita Income was introduced in 1931.

VKRV Rao (Vijayendra Kasturi Ranga Varadraj Rao) estimated national and Per Capita Income on the basis of the combination of census of output and census of income methods.

After independence, VKRV Rao was the member of 'National Income Committee' formed in August 1949 with PC Mahalanobis as its Chairman. Another member of this committee was DR Gadgil.

The first report of National Income Committee was presented in 1951.

3. Which of the following personalities was not associated with calculating income in India's economy? *(Chap 1, Class-XI, New NCERT)*

(a) Dadabhai Naoroji
(b) William Digby
(c) RC Desai
(d) A Subramaniam

➤ *Ans.* (d)

Exp. A Subramaniam was not associated with the calculation of India's national income. He was a politician from Tamil Nadu and took part in the Quit India Movement in August 1942.

During British period, several economists estimated national income of India such as Dadabhai Naoroji (1868), William Digby (1899), VKRV Rao (1931-32) and RC Desai (1931-40).

Among all these estimates, the estimation of Dadabhai Naoroji was based on the value of the output raised by agricultural sector and then added some portion of the income earned by non-agricultural sector.

4. **National income in India is estimated by**

(Chap 2, Class-XII, New NCERT) (IAS Pre 2018)

(a) Planning Commission
(b) Central Statistical Organisation
(c) Finance Commission
(d) Indian Statistical Institute

↗ *Ans. (b)*

Exp. National income in India is estimated by Central Statistical Organisation (CSO).

However, after merger of Central Statistical Organisation (CSO) with National Sample Survey Organisation (NSSO) in 2019, the newly constituted National Statistical Office (NSO) is responsible for estimation of national income in India.

This organisation is under the administrative control of Ministry of Statistics and Programme Implementation (MoSPI).

5. **Which among the following criterion is utilised by World Bank for classifying countries into developed or developing?**

(Chap 1, Class-X, New NCERT)

(a) Purchasing Power Parity
(b) Per Capita Income
(c) National Income
(d) Gross National Income

↗ *Ans. (b)*

Exp. The criterion of Per Capita Income is utilised by World Bank for classifying countries into developed (high income) or developing (low income). It is the total income of the country divided by its total population. It is also known as average income.

6. **The national income of a country for a given period is equal to the**

(Chap 2, Class-XII, New NCERT) (IAS Pre 2013)

(a) total value of goods and services produced by the nationals.
(b) sum of total consumption and investment expenditure.
(c) sum of personal income of all individuals.
(d) money value of final goods and services produced.

↗ *Ans. (d)*

Exp. The national income of a country for a given period is equal to the money value of final goods and services produced. In India, it is calculated by using combined method consisting of product/output and income method.

7. **Which of the following pairs are incorrectly matched?**

(Chap 2, Class-X, New NCERT)

(a) Final Goods – does not undergo any further transformation.
(b) Intermediate Goods – raw material or inputs for production of other commodities.
(c) Consumer Goods – food and clothing, and services like recreation.
(d) None of the above

↗ *Ans. (d)*

Exp. None of the given pairs is incorrectly matched. Final goods is such an item that is meant for final use and will not pass through any more stages of production or transformation start with first term. These items are ready to be sold finally to the consumers for final use. e.g., readymade garments.

Intermediate goods are those that don't end up in final consumption and are not capital goods either. They are mostly used as raw materials or inputs for production of other commodities.

For example, steel sheet is an intermediate good used for making automobile.

Consumer goods are those goods like food and clothing and services like recreation that are consumed when purchased by their ultimate consumers.

8. **Consider the following statements.**

(Chap 2, Class-XII, New NCERT)

1. Depreciation is an annual allowance for damage of capital goods.
2. Depreciation does not take into account unexpected or sudden destruction of capital by accident, natural calamities or other such extraneous circumstances.

Which of the statement(s) given above is/are correct?

(a) Only 1   (b) Only 2
(c) Both 1 and 2   (d) Neither 1 nor 2

↗ *Ans. (c)*

Exp. Both the statements (1) and (2) are correct.

Depreciation is reduction in value of an asset over a period of time. For example, a machine of pen making cost is ₹ 10 lakh.

After five years of use, the cost value of the machine will reduce due to its continuous use.

Depreciation does not take into account unexpected or sudden destruction or disuse of capital by an accident, natural calamities or other extraneous circumstances.

9. The largest contributor to the gross domestic savings of India is

(Chap 2, Class-XII, New NCERT) (WBPSC Pre 2017)

(a) the household sector
(b) the private corporate sector
(c) the public sector
(d) the foreign sector

↗ *Ans.* *(a)*

Exp. The household sector is the largest contributor to gross domestic savings of India. Household savings can be divided into three parts viz-physical assets, financial assets and the unaccounted savings such as gold, silver, etc. The gross domestic savings consist of savings of household sector, private corporate sector and public sector.

10. World Development Report is published by

(Chap 1, Class-X, New NCERT) (WBPSC Pre 2017)

(a) The United Nations Organisation
(b) The Asian Development Bank
(c) The World Bank
(d) The World Trade Organisation

↗ *Ans.* *(c)*

Exp. World Development Report is published by the World Bank. This report is published annually since 1978 and provides in-depth analysis of global economic trends. Based on Per Capita Income, the World Bank classifies countries into different developmental stage in the World Development Report.

11. Match the following lists correctly and choose the correct code. *(Chap 2, Class-XII, New NCERT)*

	List I (Factors)		List II (Facts)
A.	GDP_{MP}	1.	Income earned by the factors in the form of wages, profits, rents, interest etc, within the domestic territory of country.
B.	NDP_{FC}	2.	Accounting tool developed by United Nation to measure national income.
C.	SNA_{2008}	3.	Consumption of Fixed capital.
D.	Depreciation	4.	Market value of all final goods and services produced within a domestic territory of a country measured in a year.

Codes

	A	B	C	D			A	B	C	D
(a)	2	1	3	4		(b)	4	1	2	3
(c)	3	1	4	2		(d)	1	2	3	4

↗ *Ans.* *(b)*

Exp. The correct matching is A-4, B-1, C-2, D-3.

Gross Domestic Product at Market Prices (GDP_{MP}) It is the market value of all final goods and services produced within a domestic territory of a country measured in a year. It is calculated as $GDP_{MP} = C + I + G + X - M$, Where C = private consumption, I = investment, G = purchase and $X - M$ = foreign expenditure.

Net Domestic Product at Factor Cost (NDP_{FC}) It is the income earned in the form of wages, profits, rents, interest etc, within the domestic territory of a country. It is calculated as NDP_{FC} = NDP (market price) - Net Product Taxes - Net Production Taxes.

System of National Accounts, 2008 (SNA 2008). It is an accounting tool developed by United Nations to measure national income. India shifted to this methodology in 2015.

Depreciation It is also known as consumption of fixed capital. It is an annual allowance for wear and tear of a capital goods.

12. Which of the following pairs is/are correctly matched? *(Chap 2, Class-XII, New NCERT)*

(a) Expenditure Method – Aggregate value of spending that the firms receive.
(b) Income Method – Sum total of all factor payments.
(c) Product Method – Aggregate value of final goods and services produced by firms.
(d) All the pairs are correctly matched.

↗ *Ans.* *(d)*

Exp. All the given pairs are correctly matched.

Expenditure method It is a method to calculate the national income.

When the income is being spent on the goods and services produced by the firms, it takes the form of aggregate expenditure received by the firms. In expenditure method, we can measure the uppermost flow by measuring the aggregate value spending that the firms receive for the final goods and services, which they produce.

Income method In this method of GDP estimation, sum of income earned by all factors of production in an economy is added. This method is based on the principle that all economic expenditures are equal to the total income generated by production of all economic goods and services.

Product method It is used to measure the aggregate value of final goods and services produced by all the firms.

13. **Consider the following statements.**

(Chap 2, Class XII, New NCERT)

1. Market price includes indirect taxes and government subsidies.
2. Factor cost includes government grants and subsidies.
3. Base year is also called the reference year.

Which of the statement (s) given above is/are correct?

(a) Only 3
(b) 1 and 2
(c) 2 and 3
(d) All of these

➚ *Ans.* (d)

Exp. All the given statements (1), (2) and (3) are correct. Market price refers to the actual transacted price and it includes indirect taxes (excise duty, VAT, service tax etc) and government subsidies.

The factor cost means the total cost of all factors of production consumed or used in producing a good or service. It includes government grants and subsidies, but it excludes indirect taxes.

The year against which the performance of an index is measured is called base year. It is also called the reference year.

14. **After 2015, which of the following calculations by National Statistical Office (NSO) represents the national income?** *(Chap 2, Class-XII, New NCERT)*

(a) GDP at Market Price
(b) GVA at Basic Price
(c) Both 'a' and 'b'
(d) None of these

➚ *Ans.* (c)

Exp. After 2015, the National Statistical Office (NSO) replaced GDP at factor cost with the GVA at basic prices, and the GDP at market prices, which is now called only GDP.

Gross Value Added (GVA) is the value of total output produced in the economy less the value of intermediate consumption. The basic price includes the production taxes but not product taxes.

Thus, GVA at basic prices = GVA at market price – Net product taxes. GDP at market price is the market value of all final goods and services produced within a domestic territory of a country measured in a year.

Thus, GDP_{MP} = Total production + Taxes – Subsidies.

15. **With reference to estimation of national income, which of the following statement (s) is/are correct?** *(Chap 2, Class XII, New NCERT)*

1. Land, Labour, Capital and Entrepreneurship are considered as four factors of production.
2. Spending on intermediate goods are included as final expenditure for estimation of national income.

Codes

(a) Only 1
(b) Only 2
(c) Both 1 and 2
(d) Neither 1 nor 2

➚ *Ans.* (a)

Exp. Statement (1) is correct with reference to estimation of national income as Land, Labour Capital and Entrepreneurship are considered as four factors of production. These factors include, rents, wages, interest and profits respectively. It is used to calculate national income.

Statement (2) is incorrect as spending on intermediate goods are not included as final expenditure for estimation of national income to avoid the problem of double counting. These goods (such as tyres) are used for manufacturing of final products. e.g., cars.

16. **Which of the following gives an idea about the maximum amount of goods and services the domestic economy has at its disposal?** *(Chap 2, Class-XII, New NCERT)*

(a) Private Income
(b) National Disposable Income
(c) National Income
(d) None of the above

➚ *Ans.* (b)

Exp. National Disposable Income gives an idea of what is the maximum amount of goods and services the domestic economy has at its disposal.

National Disposable Income = Net National Product at market prices + Other current transfers from the rest of the world.

17. **Which of the following is/are not included in the calculation of national income?** *(Chap 3, Class-XII, Old NCERT)*

1. transfer payment by the government
2. private transfers
3. production for self-consumption

Codes

(a) 1 and 3
(b) 1 and 2
(c) 2 and 3
(d) None of the above

➚ *Ans.* (d)

Exp. All the given options are not included in the calculation of national income.

National Income or Net National Product at factor cost = NNP at market prices– (Indirect taxes – subsidies)

Thus, transfer payment by the government, private transfers and production for self-consumption are not included in national income.

18. If we deduct the Personal Tax Payments and Non-tax Payments from Personal Income, we obtain, which of the following?

(Chap 2, Class-XII, New NCERT)

(a) Personal Disposable Income
(b) Public Income
(c) National Disposable Income
(d) Per Capita Income

➚ *Ans.* (a)

Exp. If we deduct the personal income from personal tax payments and non-tax payments, then we obtain Personal Disposable Income.

Personal Disposable Income = Personal Income – Personal tax payments – Non-tax payments

Personal Disposable Income is the part of the aggregate income, which belongs to households.

19. Consider the following statements.

(Chap 2, Class XII, New NCERT)

1. The profit earned by Korean-owned Hyundai car factory is included in GNP of India.
2. The change in the inventory of a firm is treated as investment.
3. GDP deflator is considered as the best tool to measure change of prices in an economy as it includes all goods and services.

Which of the statements given above are correct?

(a) 1 and 2　　　　(b) 2 and 3
(c) 1 and 3　　　　(d) All of these

➚ *Ans.* (b)

Exp. Statements (2) and (3) are correct. The unsold stock of goods and materials is known as inventory and treated as capital. Addition to the stock of capital of a firm is known as investment. Therefore, change in the inventory of a firm is treated as investment. The reason why GDP deflator (Implicit Price Deflator) is considered as the best tool to measure change of prices in an economy as it includes all goods and services.

Statement (1) is incorrect as Gross National Product (GNP) measures the total value of all finished goods and services produced by a country's citizen in a given financial year, irrespective of their location. Therefore, profit earned by Korean-owned Hyundai car factory is included in Korean GNP.

20. Consider the following statements.

(Chap 2, Class-XII, New NCERT)

1. Nominal GDP is calculated in a way such that, the goods and services are evaluated at some constant set of prices.
2. Real GDP, on the other hand, is simply the value of GDP at the current prevailing prices.

Which of the statement(s) given above is/are correct?

(a) Only 1　　　　(b) Only 2
(c) Both 1 and 2　　(d) Neither 1 nor 2

➚ *Ans.* (d)

Exp. Neither statement (1) nor (2) is correct. Nominal GDP is the value of GDP at the current prevailing prices, on the other hand, real GDP is calculated in a way such that goods and services are evaluated at some constant set of prices or constant prices. Since, these prices remain fixed, if the real GDP changes, we can be sure that it is the volume of production which is undergoing the changes. The ratio of nominal GDP to real GDP gives us an idea of how the prices have moved from the base year to the current year.

21. The ratio of nominal to real GDP is a well-known index of prices. What is the price index known as?

(Chap 2, Class-XII, New NCERT)

(a) Consumer Price Index　　(b) GDP Deflator
(c) Wholesale Price Index　　(d) None of these

➚ *Ans.* (b)

Exp. The ratio of nominal to real GDP is a well-known index of prices. This is called GDP Deflator. If GDP stands for nominal GDP and gdp stands for real GDP,

then, GDP Deflator $= \dfrac{\text{GDP}}{\text{gdp}}$

Sometimes, GDP Deflator is also denoted in percentage terms.

In such a case, GDP deflator $= \dfrac{\text{GDP}}{\text{gdp}} \times 100$

22. Consider the following statements.

(Chap 2, Class-XII, New NCERT)

1. If the GDP of the country is rising, welfare always arises as a consequence.
2. If we relate welfare improvement in the country to the percentage of people who are better off, then GDP is not a good index.

Which of the statement(s) given above is/are incorrect?

(a) Only 1　　　　(b) Only 2
(c) Both 1 and 2　　(d) Neither 1 nor 2

➚ *Ans.* (a)

Exp. Only statement (1) is incorrect because if the GDP of the country is rising, the welfare may not rise as a consequence. This is because the rise in GDP may be concentrated in the hands of very few individuals or firms. For the rest, the income may infact have fallen.

In such a case, the welfare of the entire country cannot be said to have increased.

23. Consider the following statements.

(Chap 2, Class-XII, New NCERT)

1. The year whose prices are being used to calculate the real GDP is known as the Base Year.
2. The prices calculated at base year is known as Basic Price.

Which of the statement(s) given above is/are correct?

(a) Only 1   (b) Only 2
(c) Both 1 and 2   (d) Neither 1 nor 2

↗ *Ans.* (c)

Exp. Both the statements (1) and (2) are correct.

The year whose prices are being used to calculate the real GDP is known as the 'Base Year'. As of October, 2021, the base year for GDP in India is 2011-12. The prices calculated at base year is known as Basic Price.

24. The term 'Hindu Rate of Growth' was coined by

(Chap 2, Class XII, New NCERT)

(a) JN Bhagwati
(b) KN Raj
(c) Raj Krishna
(d) Sukhamoy Chakravarty

↗ *Ans.* (c)

Exp. Professor Raj Krishna, an Indian economist, coined the term 'Hindu Rate of Growth'. The Hindu Rate of Growth is a term referring to the low annual growth rate of the planned economy of India before the liberalisations of 1991.

The term was coined in 1978 for describing the slow growth and explaining it against the backdrop of socialistic economic policies. It is related to GDP.

25. The part of profit, which is not distributed among the factors of production is called

(Chap 2, Class-XII, New NCERT)

(a) Undistributed profits
(b) Marginal profits
(c) Rational profits
(d) Absolute profits

↗ *Ans.* (a)

Exp. Undistributed profits is a part of profit, which is not distributed among the factors of production.

Out of National Income (that is earned by the firms) and government enterprises, a part of profit not distributed among the factors of production is called as undistributed profits. In order to arrive at Personal Income (PI), we have to deduct undistributed profits from National Income, since undistributed profits does not accrue to the households.

26. Match the following lists correctly and choose the correct code.

(Chap 2, Class-XII, New NCERT)

List I (Income Determinant)	List II (Description)
A. Marginal propensity to consume	1. Change in consumption per unit change in income
B. Marginal propensity to save	2. Change in savings per unit change in income
C. Average propensity to consume	3. Consumption expenditures per unit of disposable income
D. Average propensity to save	4. Savings per unit of income

Codes

	A	B	C	D			A	B	C	D
(a)	1	2	3	4		(b)	4	3	2	1
(c)	1	3	2	4		(d)	1	2	4	3

↗ *Ans.* (a)

Exp. The correct matching is A-1, B-2, C-3, D-4.

Marginal propensity to consume It is the change in consumption per unit change in income. In other words, it is the proportion of an aggregate raise in pay that a consumer spends on the consumption of goods and services, as opposed to saving it.

Marginal propensity to save It is the change in saving per unit change in income. In other words, it is the fraction of an increase in income that is not spent and instead used for saving.

Average propensity to consume It is the consumption expenditures per unit of disposable income.

Average propensity to save It is the saving per unit of income. It is usually expressed as a percentage of total household disposable income.

27. Consider the following statements.

(Chap 2, Class-XII, New NCERT)

1. Externalities refer to the benefits or harms a firm or an individual causes to another for which they are not paid or penalised.
2. Externalities do not have any market in which they can be bought and sold.

Which of the statement(s) given above is/are correct?

(a) Only 1   (b) Only 2
(c) Both 1 and 2   (d) Neither 1 nor 2

↗ *Ans.* (c)

Exp. Both the statements (1) and (2) are correct.

Externalities refer to the benefits or harms a firm or an individual causes to another for which they are not paid. Externalities do not have any market in which they can be bought and sold.

For example, there is oil refinery which refines crude oil and sells it in the market. The output of refinery is the amount of oil it refines. The value added of the refinery will be counted as part of GDP.

But in carrying out the production it will inflict some harmful effects, for which it will not bear any cost. Such an effect is called externalities, which may be positive or negative.

28. **According to whose rule of the market forces, "supply creates its own demand"?**

(Chap 5, Class-XII, Old NCERT)

(a) Jean-Baptiste Say   (b) JM Keynes
(c) Adam Smith   (d) None of these

↗ *Ans.* *(a)*

Exp. Jean-Baptiste Say gave the rule of market forces, which stated that 'supply creates its own demand.' According to him, whatever is produced is sold in economy. There is no over or under production.

He claimed that the production of a product creates demand for another product by providing something of value which can be exchanged for that other product.

He further claimed "if certain goods remain unsold, it is because other goods are not produced."

29. **Which of the following elements does not affect investments negatively in an economy?**

(Chap 5, Class-XII, Old NCERT)

(a) Increase in marketable products
(b) Decrease in interest rates
(c) Increase in interest rates
(d) None of the above

↗ *Ans.* *(b)*

Exp. Decrease in interest rates do not affect investment negatively in an economy.Investment is inversely related to interest rates. Typically higher interest rate reduces investment, because higher rates increase the cost of the borrowing and require investment to have a higher rate of return to be profitable. On the other hand, low interest rate increases the investment and it affects the investment positively in an economy.

30. **Which of the following is/are the component(s) of aggregate demand in an economy?**

(Chap 5, Class-XII, Old NCERT)

(a) Consumption
(b) Public Expenditure
(c) Investment
(d) All of the above

↗ *Ans.* *(d)*

Exp. Consumption, public expenditure and investment all are the components of aggregate demand in an economy. Aggregate demand measures the total amount of demand of all final goods and services produced in an economy. Aggregate demand is expressed as the total amount of money exchanged for those goods and services at a specific price level and point of time.

03

Economic Planning

Old NCERT Class IX & X (The State and Economic Development),
New NCERT Class XI (Indian Economy)

1. The concept of Five Year Plans in India was borrowed from which of the following countries?

(Chap 2, Class-XI, New NCERT)

(a) USA
(b) Soviet Union
(c) Ireland
(d) Germany

↗ *Ans.* *(b)*

Exp. The concept of Five Year Plans in India was borrowed from the former Soviet Union. The plan spells out how the resources of a nation should be put to use. It laid down the roadmap for the development in India. The main purpose of Five Year Plans was to specify the objectives to be attained during the time frame of a plan. Thus, Five Year Plans were supposed to provide the basis for the perspective plan or long-term plan.

At present, Five Year Plans have been replaced with 15-year Vision Document by NITI Aayog.

2. Consider the following statements.

(Chap 5, Class-IX & X, Old NCERT)

1. In 1951, the Planning Commission was set up with the Prime Minister as its Chairperson.
2. The goals of the Five Year Plans were growth, modernisation, self-reliance and equity.

Which of the statement(s) given above is/are incorrect?

(a) Only 1
(b) Only 2
(c) Both 1 and 2
(d) Neither 1 nor 2

↗ *Ans.* *(a)*

Exp. Statement (1) is incorrect as the Planning Commission was set up in 1950 with the Prime Minister as its Chairperson. After the Constitution of Planning Commission, the era of Five Year Plans began.

3. In India, when was economic planning started?

(Chap 2, Class XI, New NCERT) (BPSC Pre 2008)

(a) 15th August, 1947
(b) 7th April, 1951
(c) 26th January, 1949
(d) 1st May, 1956

↗ *Ans.* *(c)*

Exp. In India, economic planning was started on 26th January, 1949. In 1950, the Planning Commission was set up with the Prime Minister as its Chairperson and the first Five Year Plan was launched in 1951. The economic planning upto 1990 was influenced by socialist outlook and adopted mixed economy with active participation of private sector.

4. Consider the following statements with respect to the objective of planning.

(Chap 5, Class-IX & X, Old NCERT)

1. To achieve steady and controlled growth in the economy.
2. To control and coordinate the system for the purpose of better allocation of the resources of the country.

Which of the statement(s) given above is/are correct?

(a) Only 1
(b) Only 2
(c) Both 1 and 2
(d) Neither 1 nor 2

↗ *Ans.* *(c)*

Exp. Both the statements (1) and (2) are correct with respect to the objective of planning.

The objective of the planning is to achieve steady and controlled growth in the economy. In economics, growth refers to increase in the country's capacity to produce the output of goods and services within the country.

The other objective of planning is to control and coordinate the system for the better allocation of resources of the country.

5. **Mahalanobis Plan Model adopted in India in the mid-fifties aimed at**

(Chap 2, Class-XI, New NCERT) (BPSC Pre 2015)

(a) building a strong defense industry.

(b) setting-up heavy industries, which were capital intensive.

(c) curbing inflation in the economy.

(d) removing unemployment within a short period.

↗ *Ans.* (b)

Exp. Mahalanobis Plan Model adopted in India in the mid-fifties (i.e. 1956-61) aimed at setting-up heavy industries, which were capital intensive.

This strategy provided the blueprint for Second Five Year Plan and laid down the path of industralisation in India. The Industrial Policy Resolution, 1956 aimed towards promoting industries in the backward regions of the country.

6. **With reference to Prasanta Chandra Mahalanobis, which of the given statements are correct?** *(Chap 2, Class-XI, New NCERT)*

1. He is considered as the architect of Planning in India.

2. The Second Five Year Plan was based on his ideas.

3. He established the Indian Statistical Institute (ISI) in New Delhi.

Codes

(a) 1 and 2   (b) 2 and 3

(c) 1 and 3   (d) 1, 2 and 3

↗ *Ans.* (a)

Exp. Statements (1) and (2) are correct regarding Prasanta Chandra Mahalanobis.

The Second Five Year Plan of India was based on his ideas and he laid down the roadmap for economic planning, which was followed till Eighth Five Year Plan. The Second Five Year Plan and Industrial Policy of 1957 were drafted under his leadership and it laid down the blueprint of industrialisation and development in India. Therefore, he is referred as the architect of planning in India.

Statement (3) is incorrect as PC Mahalanobis established the Indian Statistical Institute (ISI) at Calcutta (not New Delhi) and he also started a journal 'Sankhya', which still serves as a respected forum for statisticians to discuss their ideas.

7. **The decision to develop the Indian economy on socialist lines led to the policy of the government controlling the commanding heights of the economy was put forward by which of the following Five Year Plans?**

(Chap 2, Class-XI, New NCERT)

(a) First FYP   (b) Second FYP

(c) Third FYP   (d) None of these

↗ *Ans.* (b)

Exp. The decision to develop the Indian economy on socialist lines led to the policy of the government controlling the commanding heights of the economy was put forward by Second Five Year Plan (1951-56). This meant that the government would have complete control of those industries that were vital for the economy. According to this plan, the policies of private sector would have to be complimentary to those of the public sector, with public sector leading the way.

8. **Consider the following statements with respect to planning and self-reliance.**

(Chap 2, Class-XI, New NCERT)

1. A nation can promote economic growth and modernisation by using its own resources or by using resources imported from other nations.

2. The first Seven Five Year Plans gave importance to self-reliance, which means avoiding imports of those goods, which could be produced in India itself.

Which of the statement(s) given above is/are correct?

(a) Only 1

(b) Only 2

(c) Both 1 and 2

(d) Neither 1 nor 2

↗ *Ans.* (c)

Exp. Both the statements (1) and (2) are correct with respect to planning and self-reliance.

Self-reliance was one of the main objective of Five Year Plans. Self-reliance means that a nation can promote economic growth and modernisation by using its own resources or by using resources imported from other nations.

The first Seven Five Year Plans gave importance to self-reliance which means avoiding imports of those goods which could be produced in India itself.

The policy of self-reliance was considered a necessity in order to reduce our dependence on foreign countries, especially for food.

9. In the first Seven Five Year Plans, trade was characterised by an inward looking trade strategy. Technically, this strategy is called

(Chap 2, Class-XI, New NCERT)

(a) Export Substitution　　(b) Import Substitution
(c) Export Elimination　　(d) Import Elimination

↗ *Ans.* *(b)*

Exp. In the first Seven Five Year Plans, (1985-90) trade was characterised by an inward looking trade strategy and technically, this strategy is called 'Import Substitution'.

This policy aimed at replacing or substituting imports with domestic production. For example, instead of importing vehicles made in a foreign country, industries would be encouraged to produce them in India itself. In this policy, the government protected the domestic industries from foreign competition.

10. With reference to the 'Perspective Plan' which of the following statement(s) is/are correct?

(Chap 2, Class XI, New NCERT)

1. It was part of Indian economic planning till 2017 and specified the objectives to be attained in the period of twenty years.
2. Contrary to the Five Year Plans, it gave equal importance to all sectors of the economy.

Codes

(a) Only 1　　(b) Only 2
(c) Both 1 and 2　　(d) Neither 1 nor 2

↗ *Ans.* *(a)*

Exp. Statement (1) is correct with reference to the 'Perspective Plan' because it was part of Indian economic planning till 2017. It was a long-term plan which specified the objectives of the economy to be attained in the period of twenty years. The Five Year Plans provided the basis for the Perspective Plan.

Statement (2) is incorrect as in economy, different sectors are competing with each other for limited resources. Further the objectives of planning viz growth, modernisation, self-reliance, etc are itself contradictory. It resulted in the government giving more emphasis to some particular sector.

11. Consider the following statements with respect to the Seventh Five Year Plan.

(Chap 2, Class-XI, New NCERT)

1. The proportion of GDP contributed by the industrial sector increased from 13% in 1950-51 to 24.6% in 1990-91.
2. However, Indian industry was restricted largely to cotton textiles and jute.

Which of the statement(s) given above is/are correct?

(a) Only 1　　(b) Only 2
(c) Both 1 and 2　　(d) Neither 1 nor 2

↗ *Ans.* *(a)*

Exp. Only statement (1) is correct with respect to Seventh Five Year Plan.

During the first Seventh Five Year Plans important policies promoting growth of industrial sector was adopted. Notable among them were Industrial Policy Resolution of 1956, Import Substitution Policy and establishment of capital intensive heavy industries. Due to this, the proportion of GDP contributed by the industrial sector increased from 13% in 1950-51 to 24.6% in 1990-91. The rise in the industry's share during this period is an important indicator of development.

Statement (2) is incorrect as during Seventh Five Year Plan, Indian industry was not restricted only to cotton textiles and jute but to other industrial sector also. It became well diversified by 1990. There were development of many industries like automobile, electronics, telecommunication services, etc. during this period.

12. Which of the following sector's contribution to India's Gross Domestic Product decreased from first to Seven Five Year Plans between 1951 and 1990? *(Chap 2, Class-XI, New NCERT)*

(a) Agriculture Sector　　(b) Service Sector
(c) Industry Sector　　(d) All of these

↗ *Ans.* *(a)*

Exp. Agriculture sector's contribution to India's GDP decreased in the first Seven Five Year Plans between 1951 and 1990.

This is because by that time industrial and service sector started growing (1984-85), while the growth in agriculture was stagnant, which lead to the decrease in agricultural contribution to GDP. The contribution of agriculture in 1950-51 was 58% in GDP and in 1984-85 it was 36.86%.

13. Which of the following statement is not one of the outcomes of the first Seven Five Year Plans?

(Chap 2, Class-XI, New NCERT)

(a) India became self-sufficient in food production.
(b) Land reforms resulted in abolition of the hated zamindari system.
(c) In the industrial sector, the performance of public sector enterprises was satisfactory.
(d) Excessive government regulation prevented growth of entrepreneurship.

↗ **Ans.** (c)

Exp. Statement (c) is not considered as the outcome of the first Seven Five Year Plans.

Inspite of the contribution made by the public sector to the growth of Indian economy, some economists were concerned about the performance of many public sector enterprises, during first Seven Five Years Plan. It was because after four decades of planned development, no distinction was made between the individual potential of the public and the private sector.

Many public sector firms incurred huge loss during that period but continued to function because it was difficult to close a government undertaking even if it was a drain on nation's limited resources.

14. Economic schemes like Skill Training in Industries, Stationery and Books for children were started for the first time in which of the following Five Year Plans?

(Chap 5, Class-IX & X, Old NCERT)

(a) First FYP (b) Second FYP
(c) Fifth FYP (d) Sixth FYP

↗ **Ans.** (c)

Exp. Some economic schemes like Skill Training in Industries, Stationery and Books for Children were started for the first time during Fifth Five Year Plan (1974-78).

Industrial training institutes were constituted for imparting training to the workers.

20-points programme was launched during this Five Year Plan. There were three components of Socio-economic Programmes under 20-points Programme.

These were as follows

- Provisions of books and stationery to students at cheaper rates.
- Supply of essential commodities to hostel students at subsidised prices.
- Expansion of apprenticeship programme.

15. In the context of India's Five Year Plans, a shift in pattern of industrialisation with lower emphasis on the heavy industry and move on infrastructure began in *(Chap 5, Class IX & X, Old NCERT) (IAS Pre 2010)*

(a) Fourth Plan (b) Sixth Plan
(c) Eighth Plan (d) Tenth Plan

↗ **Ans.** (c)

Exp. The Eighth Five Year Plan witnessed a shift in pattern of industrialisation with lower emphasis on the heavy industry and move on infrastructure. It was operationalised between 1992 and 1997. Several new initiatives such as adoption of New Economic Policy, and promotion of foreign trade was adopted in this plan. Liberalisation, Privatisation and Globalisation as policy measures were introduced through this plan. To promote faster economic growth, government also started channelising resources into the infrastructure sector.

16. With reference to the Eighth Five Year Plan, which of the following statements are correct?

(Chap 5, Class-IX & X, Old NCERT)

1. It was continued from April 1992 to March 1997.
2. It started the practice of indicative planning in India.
3. Under this plan, government introduced an agricultural strategy which gave rise to Green revolution in India.

Codes

(a) 1 and 2 (b) 2 and 3
(c) 1 and 3 (d) All of these

↗ **Ans.** (a)

Exp. Statements (1) and (2) are correct. The period of Eighth Five Year Plan was from April, 1992 to March, 1997. This plan was based on the principles of Liberalisation, Privatisation and Globalisation. It also started the practice of indicative planning in India. This plan was launched on the backdrop of balance of payment crisis in India.

Statement (3) is incorrect as Third Five Year Plan (not Eighth Five Year Plan) introduced an agricultural strategy which gave rise to Green Revolution in India.

17. The period of the Twelfth Five Year Plan was

(Chap 2, Class-XI, New NCERT) (MPPSC Pre 2017)

(a) 2007-2012 (b) 2012-2017
(c) 2010-2015 (d) 2006-2011

↗ **Ans.** (b)

Exp. The period of the Twelfth Five Year Plan was from 2012 to 2017. This plan focussed on faster, more inclusive and sustainable growth. It was India's last Five Year Plan. The government intended to achieve 8% of GDP growth rate for the plan period. It also intended to reduce poverty by 10% during the plan period.

04

Demography, Poverty and Unemployment

New NCERT Class IX (People as a Resource), New NCERT Class IX (Poverty as a Challenge),
Old NCERT Class IX & X (An Overview of the Indian Economy), New NCERT Class X (Sectors of Indian
Economy), New NCERT Class X (Development), New NCERT Class X (Food Security in India),
New NCERT Class XI (Indian Economy on the Eve of Independence Poverty), New NCERT Class XI
(Empolyment : Growth, Information and Other Issues), New NCERT Class XI (Poverty),
New NCERT Class XI (Comparative Analysis of India and Its Neighbouring Countries)

Demography

1. Which of the following bodies is responsible for conducting census in India?

(Chap 2, Class-IX, New NCERT)

(a) Central Statistical Organisation
(b) National Sample Survey Organisation
(c) Office of the Registrar General
(d) None of the above

➚ *Ans.* *(c)*

Exp. Office of the Registrar General of India is responsible for conducting census in India after every 10 years. This office was established in 1961 for conducting censuses as well as linguistic survey in India. The position of Registrar is usually held by a civil servant holding the rank of Joint Secretary. This department comes under the Ministry of Home Affairs.

2. With reference to demography of India, which of the following statements are correct?

(Chap 1, Class-XI, New NCERT)

1. The very first census of British India was conducted in 1881.
2. The second stage of demographic transition began after 1921.
3. The overall literacy level was less than 16% at the time of independence.

Codes
(a) 1 and 2   (b) 2 and 3   (c) 1 and 3   (d) 1, 2 and 3

➚ *Ans.* *(d)*

Exp. All the statements (1), (2) and (3) are correct regarding demography of India. The very first census of British India was conducted in 1881. Though suffering from certain limitations, it revealed the unevenness in India's population growth. The second stage of demographic transition began after 1921. The year 1921 is often related to as year of great divide; the last period in which India's population declined. Between 1921 to 1951, growth rate of India's population was high. The overall literacy rate was less than 16% at the time of independence. Out of this, the female literacy rate was about 7% at a negligible low rate.

3. Consider the following statements with reference to demography of India. *(Chap 1, Class-XI, New NCERT)*

1. Life expectancy has increased from 32 years to 69 years from 1947 to 2020.
2. The Infant Mortality Rate has been reduced by around 6 times from independence till date.

Which of the statement(s) given above is/are correct?
(a) Only 1   (b) Only 2
(c) Both 1 and 2   (d) Neither 1 nor 2

➚ *Ans.* *(c)*

Exp. Both the statements (1) and (2) are correct with reference to demography of India.

In India, life expectancy has increased from 32 years to 69 years from 1947 to 2020. Life expectancy refers to the number of years an individual is expected to live based on statistical average. Infant Mortality Rate is the number of deaths per 1,000 live births of children under one year of age. Infant Mortality Rate in India by the year 2020 was around 30 per 1000 live births.

4. **What was the child sex ratio and adult sex ratio of India as per the census 2011?**

(Chap 1, Class-XI, New NCERT)

(a) 915 and 934   (b) 919 and 943
(c) 945 and 936   (d) 925 and 945

➚ *Ans. (b)*

Exp. As per census 2011, the child sex ratio and adult sex ratio in India is 919 and 943 respectively.

Child sex ratio is defined as the number of females per 1000 males in the age group of 0-6 years in a human population. On the other hand, sex ratio is defined as the number of females per 1,000 males in the population.

5. **Which of the following statements best describes Infant Mortality Rate?** *(Chap 1, Class-X, New NCERT)*

(a) It is the number of infant deaths for every 1,000 live births before completing 1 year.
(b) It is the number of infant deaths for every 1,000 live births before completing 5 years.
(c) It is the number of infant deaths for every 100 live births before completing 1 year.
(d) It is the number of infant deaths for every 100 live births before completing 5 years.

➚ *Ans. (a)*

Exp. Statement (a) best describes Infant Mortality Rate.

Infant Mortality Rate indicates the number of children that die before the age of one year as a proportion of 1,000 live children born in that particular year.

Infant mortality in India is around 30 to 35 per 1000 live births.

6. **As per the Census 2011, which state has the lowest literacy rate?** *(Chap 1, Class-X, New NCERT)*

(a) Uttar Pradesh   (b) Odisha
(c) West Bengal   (d) Bihar

➚ *Ans. (d)*

Exp. As per Census 2011, Bihar has the lowest literacy rate. The literacy rate of Bihar is 61.80% on the other hand, Kerala has the highest literacy rate 94% as per Census 2011. The literacy rate of Uttar Pradesh, Odisha and West Bengal is 67.68%, 72.87% and 76.26% respectively.

Literacy rate measures the proportion of literate population in the age group of 7 or more. The literacy rate of India, as per Census 2011, is 74.04%.

A person aged seven or above, who can both read and write with an understanding of any language, is treated as literate.

7. **Identify the incorrect statement.**

(Chap 2, Class-IX, New NCERT)

(a) Birth rate is the number of babies born for every 1,000 people during a particular period of time.
(b) Death rate is the number of people per 1,000 who die during a particular period of time.
(c) The literacy rates have increased from 18% in 1951 to 74% in 2011.
(d) None of the above

➚ *Ans. (d)*

Exp. None of the given statement is incorrect.

Birth rate, is the number of babies born for every 1,000 people during a particular period of time. As per 2020 estimate, the birth rate in India is 18.2 births per thousand population.

Death rate is the number of people per 1,000 who die during a particular period of time. As per 2020 estimate, death rate in India is 7.3 deaths per thousand population.

The literacy rates have increased from 18.32% in 1951 to 74.04% in 2011. It was highest in Kerala and lowest in Bihar. Lakshadweep is the most literate Union Territory of India.

8. **Consider the following statements with respect to literacy rate in India.** *(Chap 2, Class-IX, New NCERT)*

1. Literacy among males is nearly 14.4% higher than females.
2. It is about 4.2% higher in urban areas as compared to rural areas.

Which of the statements given above is/are correct?

(a) Only 1   (b) Only 2
(c) Both 1 and 2   (d) Neither 1 nor 2

➚ *Ans. (a)*

Exp. Statement (1) is correct with respect to literacy rate in India. Literacy rate among males is nearly 14.4% higher than females.

Statement (2) is incorrect as in urban areas literacy rate is about 14.2% and not 4.2% higher as compared to rural areas.

9. **Consider the following Assertion (A) and Reason (R) and choose the correct code.**

(Chap 2, Class-IX, New NCERT)

Assertion (A) The quality of the population ultimately decides the growth rate of the country.

Reason (R) The quality of population depends upon the literacy rate, health of a person indicated by life expectancy and skill formation acquired by the people of the country.

Codes
(a) Both A and R are true and R is the correct explanation of A.
(b) Both A and R are true, but R is not the correct explanation of A.
(c) A is true, but R is false.
(d) A is false, but R is true.

↗ *Ans.* *(a)*

Exp. Both Assertion (A) and Reason (R) are true and Reason (R) is the correct explanation of Assertion (A).

The quality of population determines capability of human resource of a country in ensuring the productivity, standard of living and social activities.

The factors that check quality of population can be education, health, sanitation etc. Literate and healthy persons are an asset for the country.

Poverty

10. **Before independence, who among the following thought for the first time about determining a poverty line?** *(Chap 4, Class-XI, New NCERT)*

(a) VKRV Rao   (b) Dr. Rajendra Prasad
(c) Dadabhai Naoroji   (d) Gopal Krishna Gokhale

↗ *Ans.* *(c)*

Exp. Before independence, Dadabhai Naoroji thought for the first time about determining a poverty line.

In the beginning, he used the menu for prisoner to arrive at 'jail cost of living'.

But in jails, there are only adults whereas in actual society, there are children also. Therefore, he appropriately adjusted this cost of living to arrive at the poverty line.

11. **Which of the following measures is/are considered to eradicate poverty?** *(Chap 4, Class XI, New NCERT)*

(a) Problem of distribution
(b) Stability in price level
(c) Increase in the rate of growth
(d) All of the above

↗ *Ans.* *(d)*

Exp. All the given measures are considered to eradicate poverty. The Public Distribution System (PDS) should be strengthened to remove poverty. Poor section should get food grains at subsidised rate and in ample quantities.

Stability in prices helps to remove poverty. If prices continue to rise, the poor will become more poor. Slow rate of growth is the main cause of poverty. So the growth rate must be accelerated.

12. **Absolute poverty means poverty in terms of** *(Chap 4, Class-XI, New NCERT) (IAS Pre 2018)*

(a) absolute number of people.
(b) the basic minimum calorie requirements.
(c) the prevailing price level.
(d) the absolute level of unemployment.

↗ *Ans.* *(b)*

Exp. Absolute poverty is poverty in terms of the basic minimum calorie requirements. It is a situation wherein an individual is unable to fulfill even the basic necessities for the sustenance of life such as food, clothing and shelter.

13. **What is the accepted calorie intake in rural and urban areas for determining the poverty line in India?** *(Chap 4, Class-XI, New NCERT)*

(a) 1900 and 2200 respectively
(b) 2100 and 2400 respectively
(c) 2400 and 2100 respectively
(d) 2200 and 2500 respectively

↗ *Ans.* *(c)*

Exp. The accepted calorie intake in rural and urban areas for determining the poverty line in India is 2400 and 2100 respectively. It is one of the way to determine the poverty line by the monetary value (per capita expenditure) of the minimum calorie intake.

Based on this, in 2011-12, the poverty line was defined for rural areas as consumption worth ₹ 972 and ₹ 1407 in urban areas per month. Though the government uses Monthly Per Capita Expenditure (MPCE) as proxy for income of households to identify the poor.

14. **In rural India, per capita consumption is ₹ 32 and in urban area it is ₹ 47 per day. This demarcation of the poverty line was given by** *(Chap 4, Class XI, New NCERT) (CGPSC Pre 2017)*

(a) SD Tendulkar Committee
(b) C Rangarajan Committee
(c) Montek Singh Ahluwalia Committee
(d) Yashwant Sinha Committee

↗ *Ans.* *(b)*

Exp. In rural India, per capita consumption is ₹ 32 and in urban area it is ₹ 47 per day, this demarcation of the poverty line was given by C Rangarajan Committee. This committee was constituted by Planning Commission (now NITI Aayog) in 2012 to review the methodology for poverty estimation in India.

According to this committee, poverty line is estimated as monthly per capita expenditure of ₹ 1407 in urban areas and ₹ 972 in rural areas.

15. **Which of the following factors contribute to poverty in India?** *(Chap 3, Class-IX, New NCERT)*

1. Landlessness
2. Unemployment
3. Size of families
4. Illiteracy

Codes
(a) 1 and 4
(b) 1, 2 and 3
(c) 1 and 2
(d) 1, 2, 3 and 4

➤ *Ans. (d)*

Exp. Landlessness, unemployment, size of families, illiteracy, social exclusion, lack of infrastructure, etc., are the factors that contribute to poverty in India. It is illiteracy and not literacy, which contribute to poverty in India. A large number of rural poor are either landless or small farmers having small holding and the income from these small holdings is not sufficient to meet the family's basic requirements. Unemployment or underemployment and the casual and intermittent nature of work in both urban and rural areas cause poverty. Larger the size of family, larger will be the expenditure, which ultimately results into poverty.

16. **Which of the following statements is/are incorrect regarding poverty?**
(Chap 3, Class-IX, New NCERT)

(a) A person is considered poor if his or her income or consumption level falls below a given 'minimum level' necessary to fulfill the basic needs.
(b) A common method used to measure poverty is based on the income or consumption level.
(c) Poverty line does not vary with time and place.
(d) None of the above

➤ *Ans. (c)*

Exp. Statement (c) is incorrect regarding poverty as poverty line may vary with time and place as what is necessary to satisfy the basic needs is different at different times and in different countries.

Therefore, each country uses an imaginary line that is considered appropriate for its existing level of development and its accepted minimum social norms.

17. **Consider the following statements about vulnerability.** *(Chap 3, Class-IX, New NCERT)*

1. Vulnerability to poverty is a measure, which describes the lesser probability of certain communities or individuals of becoming, or remaining, poor in the coming years.
2. Vulnerability is determined by the options available to different communities for finding an alternative mode of living in terms of assets, education, health and job opportunities.

Which of the statement(s) given above is/are incorrect?
(a) Only 1
(b) Only 2
(c) Both 1 and 2
(d) Neither 1 nor 2

➤ *Ans. (a)*

Exp. Statement (1) is incorrect about vulnerability. Vulnerability to poverty is a measure, which describes the greater (not lesser) probability of certain communities (e.g., Backward class) or individuals (e.g., widow or a physically handicapped person) of becoming or remaining poor in the coming years.

Thus, the proportion of people Below Poverty Line is also not the same for all social groups and economic categories in India. Social groups which are most vulnerable to poverty are SCs, STs, rural agricultural labour, households, urban casual workers, etc

18. **Consider the following statements.**
(Chap 3, Class-IX, New NCERT)

1. To determine the poverty line in India, a minimum level of food requirement, clothing, footwear, fuel and light, educational and medical requirement, etc., are determined for subsistence.
2. The present formula for food requirement while estimating the poverty line is based on the desired daily expenditure.

Which of the statement(s) given above is/are incorrect?
(a) Only 1
(b) Only 2
(c) Both 1 and 2
(d) Neither 1 nor 2

➤ *Ans. (b)*

Exp. Statement (2) is incorrect as the present formula for food requirement while estimating the poverty line is based on the desired calorie requirement (not desired daily expenditure). Food items, such as, cereals, pulses, vegetable, milk, oil, sugar, etc., together provide these needed calories. The calorie needs vary depending on age, sex and the type of work a person does.

The accepted average calorie requirement in India is 2400 calorie per person per day for rural areas and 2100 calorie per person per day for urban areas.

19. **Which of the following statements is/are incorrect regarding poverty estimation?**
(Chap 3, Class-IX, New NCERT)

(a) Despite less calorie requirement, the higher amount for urban areas has been fixed because of high prices of many essential products in urban centres.
(b) The poverty line is estimated periodically by conducting sample surveys by the Central Statistical Organisation (CSO).

(c) For making comparisons between developing countries, the World Bank uses a uniform standard for the poverty line.

(d) None of the above

↗ **Ans.** *(b)*

Exp. Statement (b) is incorrect regarding poverty estimation. The poverty line is estimated periodically by conducting sample surveys. These surveys are conducted by National Sample Survey Organisation (NSSO) normally in every five years. In 2019, NSSO was merged with Central Statistical Organisation (CSO) to constitute a unified body called National Statistical Office (NSO). Poverty estimation in India is carried out by NITI Aayog.

For the year 2011-12, the poverty line for a person was fixed at ₹ 947 per month for rural areas and ₹ 1407 for urban areas.

20. When the number of poor is estimated as the proportion of people below the poverty line, it is known as which of the following?

(Chap 4, Class-XI, New NCERT)

(a) Head Count Ratio   (b) Poverty Ratio

(c) BPL Ratio   (d) None of these

↗ **Ans.** *(a)*

Exp. When the number of poor is estimated as the proportion of people below the poverty line, it is known as 'Head Count Ratio'. It is estimated on the basis of consumption expenditure data collected by National Statistical Office (NSO). It is the population that exists or lives, below poverty threshold.

21. Match the following lists and choose the correct code. *(Chap 4, Class-XI, New NCERT)*

List I (Types of Poverty)	List II (Features)
A. Chronic	1. Who are rich most of the time but sometimes have a bad luck.
B. Churning	2. Who regularly move in and out of poverty.
C. Occasionally	3. Who are always and usually poor.

Codes

	A	B	C		A	B	C
(a)	2	1	3	(b)	3	2	1
(c)	1	3	2	(d)	1	2	3

↗ **Ans.** *(b)*

Exp. The correct matching is A-3, B-2, C-1.

Chronic Poverty These are such type of poor who are always poor and those who are usually poor but who may sometimes have a little more money e.g. casual workers.

Churning Poverty These are such group of poor who regularly move in and out of poverty e.g. small farmers and seasonal workers.

Occasionally Poverty These are such type of poor who are rich most of the time but may sometimes have a patch of bad luck. They are also called as transient poor.

22. Consider the following Assertion (A) and Reason (R) and choose the correct code.

(Chap 3, Class-IX, New NCERT)

Assertion (A) Social exclusion is both a cause as well as a consequence of poverty.

Reason (R) Social exclusion is a process through which individuals or groups are excluded from facilities, benefits and opportunities that others enjoy.

Codes

(a) Both A and R are true and R is the correct explanation of A.

(b) Both A and R are true, but R is not the correct explanation of A.

(c) A is true, but R is false.

(d) A is false, but R is true.

↗ **Ans.** *(a)*

Exp. Both Assertion (A) and Reason (R) are true and Reason (R) is the correct explanation of Assertion (A). Social exclusion is both a cause as well as a consequence of poverty.

Poverty must be seen in terms of the person living in poor surrounding with other poor people, excluded from enjoying social equality of better-off people in better surroundings.

Broadly, it is a process through which individuals or groups are excluded from facilities, benefits and opportunities that other enjoy. A typical example is the working of the caste system in India in which people belonging to certain castes are excluded from equal opportunities.

23. Which of the following statements is incorrect about hunger? *(Chap 4, Class-IX, New NCERT)*

(a) Hunger is not just an expression of poverty, it brings about poverty.

(b) Chronic hunger is a consequence of diets persistently inadequate in terms of quantity and/or quality.

(c) Seasonal hunger is related to cycles of food growing and harvesting.

(d) The proportion of chronic hunger is higher than seasonal hunger.

↗ **Ans.** *(d)*

Exp. Statement (d) is incorrect about hunger as the proportion of seasonal hunger is higher than the chronic hunger. Chronic hunger is a consequence of diets persistently inadequate in terms of quantity or quality.

Poor people suffer from chronic hunger because of their low income and in turn inability to buy food even for survival. On the other hand, seasonal hunger is related to cycles of food growing and harvesting. It is prevalent in rural areas because of seasonal nature of agricultural activities and in urban areas because of casual workers.

24. Which of the following statements is incorrect regarding vulnerable groups?

(Chap 3, Class-IX, New NCERT)

(a) Social groups, which are most vulnerable to poverty, are Scheduled Castes and Scheduled Tribe households.

(b) Among the economic groups, the most vulnerable groups are the rural agricultural labour households.

(c) Although the average for people Below Poverty Line for all groups in India is 22 and 43 out of 100 people belong to the Other Backward Castes.

(d) None of the above

↗ **Ans.** *(c)*

Exp. Statement (c) is incorrect regarding vulnerable groups as the average for people Below Poverty Line (BPL) for all groups in India is 22.

43 out of 100 people belonging to Scheduled Tribes (not other Backward Castes) are not able to meet their basic need. Vulnerability to poverty is a measure, which describes the greater probability of certain communities or individuals of becoming or remaining poor in the coming years.

Some of the socially vulnerable groups are Scheduled Castes and Scheduled Tribes. On the other hand, some of the economically vulnerable groups are rural agricultural labourer, urban casual labours, etc.

25. Which of the following vulnerable groups has not seen decline in the Poverty rate in the 1990s?

(a) Scheduled Tribes   *(Chap 3, Class-IX, New NCERT)*

(b) Scheduled Castes

(c) Rural Agricultural Labourer

(d) Urban Casual Worker

↗ **Ans.** *(a)*

Exp. In the given options, Scheduled Tribes has not seen decline in poverty rate in 1990s. According to studies, except for the Scheduled Tribes households, all the other three groups (i.e.) Scheduled Castes, rural agricultural labourers and urban casual labour households have seen a decline in poverty in the 1990s.

As per estimates of poverty in India (2011-12), 43 out of 100 people belonging to STs are not able to meet their basic needs, on the other hand, 34% of casual workers in urban as well as rural areas and 29% of Scheduled Castes are also poor.

26. Consider the following statements.

1. Uttar Pradesh and Odisha continue to be the two poorest states with poverty ratios of 33.7 and 32.6% respectively.

2. The reason for higher poverty rate in Odisha, Madhya Pradesh, Bihar and Uttar Pradesh is rural poverty.   *(Chap 3, Class-IX, New NCERT)*

Which of the statement(s) given above is/are incorrect?

(a) Only 1   (b) Only 2

(c) Both 1 and 2   (d) Neither 1 nor 2

↗ **Ans.** *(c)*

Exp. Both the statements (1) and (2) are incorrect.

As per Census 2011, Bihar (not Uttar Pradesh) and Odisha continue to be the two poorest states with poverty ratio of 33.7 and 32.6% respectively. The head count ratio was 21.9% in 2011-12 in states like Madhya Pradesh, Assam, Bihar and Odisha, which was well above all India poverty line.

Along with rural poverty, urban poverty is also high in Odisha, Madhya Pradesh, Bihar and Uttar Pradesh. As per Census 2011, the poverty ratio in states such as Odisha, Madhya Pradesh, Bihar and Uttar Pradesh are 32.6%, 31.7%, 33.7% and 29.4% respectively.

27. Consider the following statements.

(Class 4, Class XI, New NCERT)

1. The global Multidimensional Poverty Index (MPI) 2018 noted that 271 million people moved out of poverty between 2005-06 and 2015-16 in India.

2. As per the UNDP, the percentage of people living below the poverty line in India as of 2011 is above 50%.

Which of the statements given above is/are correct?

(a) Only 1   (b) Only 2

(c) Both 1 and 2   (d) Neither 1 nor 2

↗ **Ans.** *(c)*

Exp. Both the statements (1) and (2) are correct. The global Multidimensional Poverty Index 2018 released by the United Nations noted that 271 million people moved out of poverty between 2015-16 in India. The poverty rate in the country has nearly halved, falling from 55% to 28% over 10 year period. As per the United Nations Development Programme (UNDP), the percentage of people living below the poverty line in India as of 2011 is 53.4%. Still a big part of the population in India is living below the poverty line.

28. Consider the following Assertion (A) and Reason (R) and choose the correct code.

(Chap 3, Class-IX, New NCERT)

Assertion (A) There is a strong link between economic growth and poverty reduction.

Reason (R) Economic growth widens opportunities and provides the resources needed to invest in human development.

Codes

(a) Both A and R are true and R is the correct explanation of A.

(b) Both A and R are true, but R is not the correct explanation of A.

(c) A is true, but R is false.

(d) A is false, but R is true.

↗ *Ans.* *(a)*

Exp. Both Assertion (A) and Reason (R) are true and Reason (R) is the correct explanation of Assertion (A). There is a strong link between economic growth and poverty reduction. As we see in case of India, official poverty estimates were 45% in 1950 and it remained the same even in the early eighties. Since, eighties India's economic growth has been one of the fastest in the world. The higher growth rate helped significantly in the reduction of poverty.

Economic growth widens opportunities and provides the resources needed to invest in human development. This also encourages people to send their children including the girl child to schools in the hope of getting better economic returns from investing in education.

29. As per the Tendulkar Methodology, what is the percentage of poor in India in 2011-12?

(Chap 3, Class-IX, New NCERT) (UPPSC Pre 2012)

(a) 21%　　(b) 23%　　(c) 22%　　(d) 25%

↗ *Ans.* *(c)*

Exp. As per the Tendulkar Methodology, the percentage of poor in India was 22% in 2011-12. As per this report, nearly 69 million (22% of the population) were below poverty line. This committee recommended using mixed reference period based estimates and consumption basket of people close to the poverty line for updating poverty lines. It is based on the consumption of the items like cereal, pulses, milk, edible oil, non-vegetarian items, etc.

30. Which of the following statement(s) is related to identification of poor in India?

(Chap 4, Class-XI, New NCERT)

(a) Planning Commission Study Group of 1962.

(b) Task Force on Projections of Minimum Needs and Effective Consumption Demand.

(c) Expert Group of 2005.

(d) All of the above

↗ *Ans.* *(d)*

Exp. All the given statements are related to identification of poor in India. In post-Independent India, there have been several attempts to work out a mechanism to identify the number of poor in the country.

For instance, in 1962, the Planning Commission, now called NITI Aayog, formed a study group. In 1979, another body called the 'Task Force on Projections of Minimum Needs and Effective Consumption Demand' was formed to identify the poor.

In 1989 and 2005, 'Expert Groups' were constituted for the same purpose.

Besides the Planning Commission, many individual economists have also attempted to develop such a mechanism.

31. Which of the following statements is incorrect about the challenges to eradicate poverty?

(Chap 3, Class-IX, New NCERT)

(a) Eradication of poverty is always a moving target.

(b) Officially, it is about a 'reasonable' subsistence level of living rather than a 'minimum' level of living.

(c) Worldwide experience shows that with development, the definition of what constitutes poverty also changes.

(d) None of the above

↗ *Ans.* *(b)*

Exp. Statement (b) is incorrect about the challenges to eradicate poverty. Officially poverty, is about a 'minimum' subsistence level of living rather than a 'reasonable' level of living. However, this definition captures only a limited part of what poverty really means to people.

As suggested by scholars, we must broaden the concept of human poverty. It should not only be confined to feeding but better education, better healthcare, job security, shelters should be included while defining poverty.

32. Consider the following Assertion (A) and Reason (R) and choose the correct code.

(Chap 2, Class-IX & X, Old NCERT)

Assertion (A) India's poverty is primarily dependent on the fact that it is not possible for it to provide a profitable employment to its very large workforce.

Reason (R) Due to being less developed, India does not have enough land and capital to meet this huge population.

Codes

(a) Both A and R are true and R is the correct explanation of A.

(b) Both A and R are true, but R is not the correct explanation of A.

(c) A is true, but R is false.

(d) A is false, but R is true.

↗ *Ans.* (a)

Exp. Both Assertion (A) and Reason (R) are true and Reason (R) is the correct explanation of Assertion (A).

India's poverty is primarily dependent on the fact that it is not possible to provide a profitable employment to its very large workforce. For instance, more than half of the workers in the country are working in primary sector and are underemployed.

India being a developing country, its does not have enough land and capital to meet huge population. In India, around 17% of world's population resides in only 2.4% of total geographical area of the world.

33. **Antyodaya Programme was started first of all in the state of** *(Chap 4, Class IX, New NCERT) (BPSC Pre 2019)*

(a) Bihar

(b) Tamil Nadu

(c) Andhra Pradesh

(d) Rajasthan

↗ *Ans.* (d)

Exp. In the year 2000, Antyodaya Programme was started from Rajasthan. This scheme focuses on 'poorest of the poor' and provides provision of 35 kg of food grains at a highly subsidised rate of ₹ 3 per kg for rice and ₹ 2 per kg for wheat. It is operated through existing Public Distribution System (PDS) networks.

34. **Which yojana is related to providing LPG connection for poor household?**

(Chap 4 ,Class IX, New NCERT)

(a) Ujala Yojana (b) NULM

(c) PMUY (d) PMGKY

↗ *Ans.* (c)

Exp. Pradhan Mantri Ujjwala Yojana (PMUY) was launched in May 2016 to provide LPG (Liquefied Petroleum Gas) connections to poor households in India.

Prime Minister Narendra Modi also launched PM Ujjwala 2.0 Yojana in August 2021. Ujjwala 2.0 will provide first refill and hot plate free of cost to the beneficiaries. In this yojana, migrants will not be required to submit ration cards or address proof. The PMUY was valid till 30th September, 2020.

35. **Identify the incorrect statements about Antyodaya Anna Yojana.** *(Chap 4, Class-IX, New NCERT)*

(a) Antyodaya Anna Yojana (AAY) was launched in December 2000.

(b) Under this scheme, one crore of the poorest among the BPL families covered under the Targeted Public Distribution System were identified.

(c) 45 kilograms of foodgrains were made available to each eligible family at a highly subsidised rate of 2 per kg for rice and 3 per kg for wheat.

(d) Poor families were identified by the respective state rural development departments through a Below Poverty Line (BPL) Survey.

↗ *Ans.* (c)

Exp. Statement (c) is incorrect about Antyodaya Anna Yojana as under Antyodaya Anna Yojana (AAY), 35 kg of foodgrains were made available to each eligible family at a highly subsidised rate of ₹ 3 per kg for rice and ₹ 2 per kg for wheat.

This scheme was launched in 2000 and under this scheme, 1 crore of the poorest among the BPL families were identified by the respective state rural development departments through a BPL Survey. This scheme has been further expanded twice by additional 50 lakh BPL families in June, 2003 and in August, 2004. With this increase, 2 crore families have been covered under AAY.

36. **Which of the following pairs is/are correctly matched?** *(Chap 3, Class IX, New NCERT)*

(a) IRDP – Subsidy and bank credit.

(b) JRY – Economic infrastructure

(c) NOAPS – Pension

(d) All of the above

↗ *Ans.* (d)

Exp. All of the given pairs are correctly matched. Integrated Rural Development Programme (IRDP) was introduced in 1978-79 and universalised from 2nd October 1980, aimed at providing assistance to the rural poor in the form of subsidy and bank credit for productive employment opportunities through successive plan periods.

The Jawahar Rozgar Yojana (JRY) was meant to generate meaningful employment opportunities for the unemployed and underemployed in rural areas through the creation of economic infrastructure and community and social assets.

National Old Age Pension Scheme (NOAPS) is given by the Central government. The amount of old age pension is ₹ 200 per month for applicants aged 60-79. For applicants aged above 80 years, the amount has been revised to ₹ 500 a month.

37. Consider the following statements about the National Food Security Act, 2013.

(Chap 4, Class-IX, New NCERT)

1. This Act provides for food and nutritional security at affordable prices and enable people to live a life with dignity.
2. Under this Act, 60% of the rural population and 50% of the urban population have been categorised as eligible households for food security.

Which of the statement(s) given above is/are incorrect?

(a) Only 1
(b) Only 2
(c) Both 1 and 2
(d) Neither 1 nor 2

↗ *Ans.* (b)

Exp. Only statement (2) is incorrect about the National Food Security Act, 2013 as under this Act, 75% of the rural population and 50% of urban population have been categorised as eligible households for food security.

38. Which of the following is not one of the three major programmes that aim at improving the food and nutritional status of the poor?

(Chap 4, Class-XI, New NCERT)

(a) Public Distribution System
(b) POSHAN Abhiyaan
(c) Midday Meal Scheme
(d) PM Adarsh Gram Yojana

↗ *Ans.* (d)

Exp. PM Adarsh Gram Yojana is not one of the three major programmes that aim at improving the food and nutritional status of the poor. Pradhan Mantri Adarsh Gram Yojana (PMAGY) is a government of India initiative for the empowerment of deprived sections, aims to achieve integrated development of selected villages through convergent implementation of all relevant Central and State schemes.

39. Which of the following statements is incorrect regarding the Public Distribution System (PDS)?

(Chap 4, Class-IX, New NCERT)

(a) From the very beginning, the coverage of PDS included the poor families only.
(b) In 1992, Revamped Public Distribution System (RPDS) was introduced in 1,700 blocks in the country with a target to provide the benefits of PDS to remote and backward areas.
(c) From June 1997, in a renewed attempt, Targeted Public Distribution System (TPDS) was introduced to adopt the principle of targeting the 'poor in all areas'.

(d) In 2000, Antyodaya Anna Yojana (AAY) and Annapurna Scheme (APS) were launched with special target groups of 'poorest of the poor' and 'indigent senior citizens', respectively.

↗ *Ans.* (a)

Exp. Statement (1) is incorrect regarding Public Distribution System (PDS). In the beginning, the coverage of PDS was universal with no discrimination between poor and non-poor. Over the years, the policy related to PDS has been revised to make it more efficient and target based. The PDS has proved to be the most effective instrument of government policy over the years in stabilising prices and making food available to consumers at affordable prices. It has been instrumental in averting widespread hunger and famine by supplying food from surplus regions of the country to the deficit ones.

Unemployment

40. Unemployment in India is concentrated in

(Chap 2, Class-IX, New NCERT) (WBPSC Pre 2020)

(a) Organised sector
(b) Unorganised sector
(c) Both organised and unorganised sectors
(d) Foreign trade sector

↗ *Ans.* (a)

Exp. Unemployment in India is concentrated in organised sector. Any sector in which the firm or organisation is registered with the government is called organised sector. People working in organised sector (also known as Formal Sector) enjoy Social Security benefits. Unorganised sector includes millions of farmers, agricultural labourers, owners of small enterprises etc.

41. Disguised unemployment refers to

(Chap 7, Class XI, New NCERT) (UPPSC Pre 2004)

(a) employment of more persons in a job which can be accomplished by lesser number of persons
(b) persons with no job
(c) unemployment among housewives
(d) unemployment among people above 60 years of age.

↗ *Ans.* (a)

Exp. Disguised unemployment refers to employment of more persons in a job which can be accomplished by lesser number of persons. This type of unemployment is most frequent in agricultural sector of India. Economists define unemployed person as one who is not able to get employment of even one hour in half a day.

42. Consider the following statements.

(Chap 7, Class XI, New NCERT)

1. Cyclical unemployment figures in India are negligible.
2. The frictional unemployment also called as search unemployment.
3. Vulnerable employment rarely found in India.

Which of the statement(s) given above is/are incorrect?

(a) 1 and 2   (b) Only 3   (c) 2 and 3   (d) 1 and 3

➚ *Ans.* (b)

Exp. Statement (3) is incorrect.

Vulnerable employment means, people working informally, without proper job contracts and thus lack any legal protection. These persons are deemed unemployed since records of their work are never maintained. It is one of the main types of unemployment in India.

Cyclic unemployment figures in India are negligible. It is a phenomenon that is mostly found in capitalist economies. The frictional unemployment is also called as Search unemployment. It refers to the time lag between the jobs when an individual is searching for a new job or is switching between the jobs.

43. Consider the following statements.

(Chap 2, Class-IX, New NCERT)

1. Unemployment is said to exist when people who are willing to work at the going wages cannot find jobs.
2. The workforce population in India includes people from 18 years to 59 years.

Which of the statement(s) given above is/are correct?

(a) Only 1   (b) Only 2
(c) Both 1 and 2   (d) Neither 1 nor 2

➚ *Ans.* (a)

Exp. Only statement (1) is correct.

Unemployment is said to exist when people who are willing to work at the going wages cannot find jobs.

The National Statistical Office (previously known as CSO) defines unemployment as a situation in which all those who, owing to lack of work, are not working but either seek work through employment exchanges, intermediaries, friends or relatives or by making applications to prospective employers or express their willingness for availability of work under the prevailing condition of work and remunerations.

Statement (2) is incorrect because the workforce population includes people from 15 years to 59 years. Thus, the persons falling between these age group are called as workforce population.

44. Consider the following Assertion (A) and Reason (R) and choose the correct code.

(Chap 2, Class-IX, New NCERT)

Assertion (A) If people cannot be used as a resource they naturally appear as a liability to the economy.

Reason (R) Unemployment has a detrimental impact on the overall growth of an economy.

Codes

(a) Both A and R are true and R is the correct explanation of A.
(b) Both A and R are true, but R is not the correct explanation of A.
(c) A is true, but R is false.
(d) A is false, but R is true.

➚ *Ans.* (a)

Exp. Both Assertion (A) and Reason (R) are true and Reason (R) is the correct explanation of Assertion (A).

If people cannot be used as a resource, they naturally appear as a liability to the economy. It wastes the resources, which could have been gainfully employed. Unemployment has a detrimental impact on the overall growth of an economy. It tends to increase economic overload. The dependence of the unemployed people on the working population increases. Increase in unemployment is also an indicator of depressed economy.

45. Which of the following statements is incorrect about unemployment?   *(Chap 2, Class-IX, New NCERT)*

(a) Seasonal unemployment happens when people are not able to find jobs during some months of the year.
(b) In case of disguised unemployment people appear to be employed but their marginal output is zero.
(c) In educated unemployment many youth with matriculation, graduation and post-graduation degrees are not able to find jobs.
(d) Urban areas mostly have seasonal and disguised unemployment.

➚ *Ans.* (d)

Exp. Statement (d) is incorrect about unemployment as in urban areas, seasonal and disguised unemployment is not seen mostly while educated unemployment has become common phenomenon. In these areas, many youth with matriculation, graduation and post-graduation degrees are not able to find the job.

A study showed that unemployment of graduate and post-graduate has increased faster than among matriculates. In urban areas, there is unemployment among technically qualified person on one hand, while there is a dearth of technical skills required for economic growth. Seasonal and disguised unemployment is mostly prevalent in rural areas.

46. Consider the following statements about worker population ratio. *(Chap 7, Class-XI, New NCERT)*

1. If the ratio is medium or low, it means that the engagement of people is greater.
2. If the ratio for a country is higher, it means that a very high proportion of its population is not involved directly in economic activities.

Which of the statement(s) given above is/are correct?

(a) Only 1
(b) Only 2
(c) Both 1 and 2
(d) Neither 1 nor 2

↗ *Ans.* (d)

Exp. Neither statement (1) nor (2) is correct about worker population ratio.

Worker population ratio is an indicator which is used for analysing the employment situation in the country. If the ratio for a country is medium or low, it means that a very high proportion of its population is not involved directly in economic activities.

If the ratio is higher, it means that the engagement of people is greater in economic activities. This ratio is also useful in knowing the proportion of population that is actively contributing to the production of goods and services of a country.

47. Which of the following statements is incorrect regarding types of employees? *(Chap 7, Class-XI, New NCERT)*

(a) Workers who own and operate an enterprise to earn their livelihood are known as self-employed.
(b) Casual workers are engaged in others' farms and, in return, get remuneration for the work done.
(c) When a worker is engaged by someone or an enterprise and paid his or her wages on a regular basis, they are known as contractual employees.
(d) None of the above

↗ *Ans.* (c)

Exp. Statement (c) is incorrect regarding types of employees. When a worker is engaged by someone or an enterprise and paid his or her wages on a regular basis, they are known as 'regular salaried employees'. In regular salaries employment, both women and men are found to be engaged in greater proportion. According to International Labour Organisation, India had 23.99% salaried employees in the year 2020.

48. Which one of the following is the objective of MGNREGA? *(Chap 3, Class-IX, New NCERT)*

(BPSC Pre 2018)

(a) to build assets
(b) to encourage micro-irrigation
(c) water management
(d) to enhance rural income

↗ *Ans.* (d)

Exp. The main objective of Mahatma Gandhi National Rural Employment Guarantee Act (MGNREGA) is to enhance rural income.

It aims to provide 100 days of wage employment to every household to ensure livelihood security in rural areas. It also aimed at Sustainable Development to address the cause of drought, deforestation and soil erosion.

49. Female workforce participation is highest in which of the following sectors of the Indian economy? *(Chap 7, Class-XI, New NCERT)*

(a) Primary
(b) Secondary
(c) Tertiary
(d) Quinary

↗ *Ans.* (a)

Exp. Female workforce participation is highest in primary sector of the Indian economy.

About 57% of the female workforce is employed in the primary sector whereas less than half of the males work in that sector.

The primary sector is concerned with the extraction of raw materials or natural resources from the land. These are also known as agricultural and allied sector services.

50. Consider the following statements. *(Chap 7, Class-XI, New NCERT)*

1. The process of moving from casual wage workforce to self-employment and regular salaried employment is known as casualisation of the workforce.
2. Casualisation of the workforce protects workers from vulnerability.

Which of the statement(s) given above is/are correct?

(a) Only 1
(b) Only 2
(c) Both 1 and 2
(d) Neither 1 nor 2

↗ *Ans.* (d)

Exp. Neither Statement (1) nor (2) is correct.

The process of moving from casual wage workforce to self-employment and regular salaried employment is not called casualisation of the workforce.

Casualisation of workforce is the process of moving from self-employment and regular salaried employment to casual wage work. Casualisation of the workforce makes the workers highly vulnerable as they are not paid on a regular basis.

51. With reference to 'employment in formal sector', which of the following statement(s) is/are correct? *(Chap 7, Class XI, New NCERT)*

1. Information relating to employment in the formal sector is collected by the Ministry of Personnel.
2. All the public sector establishments and those private sector establishments, which employ 10 hired workers or more are called formal sector establishments.

Codes
(a) Only 1
(b) Only 2
(c) Both 1 and 2
(d) Neither 1 nor 2

↗ *Ans.* *(b)*

Exp. Statement (2) is correct with reference to 'employment in formal sector'.

The criterion of 10 workers is utilised for classification of establishments into formal or informal sector. It includes both public sector as well as private sector establishments.

Statement (1) is incorrect as the information relating to employment in the formal sector is collected by the Union Ministry of Labour through employment exchanges located in different parts of the country.

52. Which of the following offices and their sources of data on unemployment is incorrectly matched? *(Chap 2, Class-X, New NCERT)*

(a) Registrar General - Reports of Census of India
(b) National Statistical Office - Reports of Employment and Unemployment Situation
(c) Central Statistical Organisation - Annual Periodic Labour Force Survey
(d) Directorate General of Employment - Registration with Employment Exchanges

↗ *Ans.* *(c)*

Exp. Pair (c) is incorrectly matched. There are three sources of data on unemployment. These are as follows :

(i) Reports of Census of India, provided by Registrar General.
(ii) Reports of Employment and unemployment situations, annual Reports of Periodic Labour Force Survey provided by National Statistical Office.
(iii) Data of Registration with employment exchanges, provided by Directorate General of Employment and Training.

53. Consider the following statements.
(Chap 4, Class IX, New NCERT)

1. Start Up India Scheme promotes entrepreneurship of SCs or STs across the country.
2. Stand Up India Scheme aims to facilitate bank loan at least one women borrower per bank branch.

Which of the statement (s) given above is/are incorrect?
(a) Only 1
(b) Only 2
(c) Both 1 and 2
(d) Neither 1 nor 2

↗ *Ans.* *(a)*

Exp. Statement (1) is incorrect. Start Up India Scheme was launched in 2016 and aims at developing an ecosystem that promotes and nurtures entrepreneurship across the country.

It was launched in 2016. Stand Up India Scheme aims to facilitate bank loans between ₹ 10 lakh and ₹ 1 crore to atleast on SC or ST borrower and at least one women borrower per bank branch for setting up a greenfield enterprise.

54. Consider the following statements.
(Chap 4, Class IX, New NCERT)

1. The NULM focuses on organising Urban poor in Self Help Groups.
2. Pradhan Mantri Kaushal Vikas Yojana focuses on labour market.
3. Pradhan Mantri Jan Dhan Yojana focuses on unbanked poor.

Which of the statement(s) given above is/are correct?
(a) 1 and 2
(b) 1, 2 and 3
(c) 2 and 3
(d) 1 and 3

↗ *Ans.* *(b)*

Exp. All the given statements (1), (2) and (3) are correct.

The National Urban Livelihood Mission (NULM) focuses on organising urban poor in Self Help Groups, creating opportunities for skill development leading to market-based employment and helping them to set up self-employment ventures by ensuring easy access to credit.

Pradhan Mantri Kaushal Vikas Yojana will focus on fresh entrants to the labour market, especially labour market and class X and XII dropouts.

Pradhan Mantri Jan Dhan Yojana aimed at direct benefit transfer of subsidy, pension, insurance etc. The scheme particularly targets the unbanked poor.

05

Rural and Urban Development and Basic Infrastructure

New NCERT Class XI (Rural Development), New NCERT Class XI (Infrastructure)

1. Which of the following is/are included in non-agricultural production activities?

(Chap 6, Class-XI, New NCERT)

1. Health Facilities
2. Education
3. Dairy
4. Food Processing
5. Small-scale manufacturing
6. Transportation

Codes
(a) 2 and 3
(b) 4, 5 and 6
(c) 1, 2, 5 and 6
(d) 1, 2, 3, 4, 5 and 6

↗ *Ans.* (d)

Exp. Health facilities, education, dairy, food processing, small-scale manufacturing and transportation are included in non-agricultural production activities. Non-farm agricultural activities are such activities which do not involve agriculture and are important for rural development.

The non-farm activities help in establishing market in the village, act as a source of income for the farmers, and also provide employment to landless labourers.

2. Consider the following statements with respect to the significance of rural development.

(Chap 6, Class-XI, New NCERT)

1. More than two-third of India's population depends on agriculture that is yet to become productive enough.
2. One-third of rural India still lives in poverty.

Which of the statement(s) given above is/are incorrect?

(a) Only 1
(b) Only 2
(c) Both 1 and 2
(d) Neither 1 nor 2

↗ *Ans.* (b)

Exp. Only statement (2) is incorrect with respect to the significance of rural development because one-fourth (not one-third) of rural India still lives in poverty.

The majority of poor live in rural areas do not have access to the basic necessities of life that is the reason we need a developed rural India, if our nation want to achieve a real progress.

3. Which of the following areas are lagging behind in the overall development of the village economy?

1. Land reforms   *(Chap 6, Class-XI, New NCERT)*
2. Infrastructure development like electricity, irrigation
3. Literacy
4. Health Infrastructure

Codes
(a) 1, 2 and 4
(b) 2 and 4
(c) 3 and 4
(d) 1, 2, 3 and 4

↗ *Ans.* (d)

Exp. All the areas given in the options are lagging behind in the overall development of the village economy. Rural development is a comprehensive term and focusses on action for development of areas that are lagging behind in the overall development of the village economy.

Some of the areas which are challenging and need new initiatives for development in rural areas are

- Land reforms like size, acquisition and distribution of agricultural land.
- Infrastructure development like electricity, irrigation, credit, marketing, transport facilities including construction of village roads to nearby highways, facilities for agriculture research and extension and information dissemination.
- Development of human resources including literacy (more specifically female literacy), skill development, health, sanitation and public health.

4. Consider the following Assertion (A) and Reason (R) and choose the correct code.

Assertion (A) Growth of rural economy depends primarily on infusion of capital, from time to time, to realise higher productivity in agricultural and non-agricultural sectors.

Reason (R) As the time of gestation between crop sowing and realisation of income after production is quite long, farmers borrow from various sources to meet their initial investment on seeds and fertilisers. *(Chap 6, Class-XI, New NCERT)*

Codes

(a) Both A and R are true and R is the correct explanation of A.

(b) Both A and R are true, but R is not the correct explanation of A.

(c) A is true, but R is false.

(d) A is false, but R is true.

↗ ***Ans.*** *(a)*

Exp. Both Assertion (A) and Reason (R) are true and Reason (R) is the correct explanation of Assertion (A). Growth of rural economy depends primarily on infusion of capital, from time to time, to realise higher productivity in agriculture and non-agriculture sectors.

It is to be noted that the time of gestation between crop sowing and realisation of income after production is quite long. As a result, farmers borrow from various sources to meet their initial investment on seeds, fertilisers etc. That's why there is a need of capital from time to time for the growth of rural economy.

5. Which one of the following is not a source of direct finance?

(Chap 6, Class-XI, New NCERT) (BPSC Pre 2015)

(a) NABARD   (b) Regional Rural Bank

(c) State Bank of India   (d) Allahabad Bank

↗ ***Ans.*** *(a)*

Exp. National Bank for Agriculture and Rural Development (NABARD) is not a source of direct finance. It was set up in 1982 as an apex body to coordinate the activities of all institutions involved in the rural financing system.

6. In India, which of the following have the highest share in the disbursement of credit to agriculture and allied activities?

(Chap 6, Class-XI, New NCERT) (IAS Pre 2001)

(a) Microfinance Institutions

(b) Regional Rural Banks

(b) Cooperative Banks

(d) Commercial Banks

↗ ***Ans.*** *(d)*

Exp. Commercial Banks have the highest share in the disbursement of credit to agriculture and allied activities.

The institutional structure of rural banking consists of a set of multi-agency institutions, namely, Commercial Banks, Regional Rural Banks, Cooperative and Land Development Banks.

7. Which of the following statements is incorrect regarding rural credit? *(Chap 6, Class-XI, New NCERT)*

(a) After 1969, India adopted the social banking and multi-agency approach to adequately meet the needs of rural credit.

(b) The NABARD was set up as a financial institution involved in the dairy activities only.

(c) The Green Revolution was a harbinger of major changes in the credit system as it led to the diversification of the portfolio of rural credit towards production-oriented lending.

(d) All are correct

↗ ***Ans.*** *(b)*

Exp. Statement (b) is incorrect regarding rural credit as the National Bank for Agriculture and Rural Development (NABARD).

It was set up in 1982 as an apex body to coordinate the activities of all institutions involved in the rural financing system.

At the time of independence, moneylenders and traders used to exploit landless labourers by lending them money on high interest rates.

Therefore, many rural credit banks like NABARD, Regional Rural Banks (RRBs) and Cooperative banks etc came into existence.

8. **Which one of the following is not the formal institution for providing the facilities for rural credit in India?** *(Chap 6, Class-XI, New NCERT)*
(a) Commercial Banks
(b) Regional Rural Banks
(c) Moneylender and merchants
(d) Cooperative and land development banks

↗ *Ans.* *(c)*

Exp. Among the given options, moneylender and merchants is not the formal institution for providing the facilities for rural credit in India. The institutional structure of rural banking today consists of a set of multi-agency institutions namely, Commercial banks, Regional Rural Banks (RRBs), Cooperatives and Land Development Banks. They are expected to dispense adequate credit at cheaper rates. Self-Help Groups (SHGs) have also emerged as a rural credit institution.

9. **'Kudumbashree' is a women-oriented community-based poverty reduction programme for rural areas being implemented in which of the following states?** *(Chap 6, Class-XI, New NCERT)*
(a) West Bengal (b) Telangana
(c) Kerala (d) Odisha

↗ *Ans.* *(c)*

Exp. 'Kudumbashree' is a women-oriented community based poverty reduction programme being implemented in Kerala. It is a thrift and credit society which mobilised 1 crore as thrift savings. In 1995, it was started as a small saving banks for poor women with the objective to encourage savings.

These societies have been acclaimed as the largest informal banks in Asia in terms of participation and savings mobilised.

10. **Consider the following statements about Self-Help Groups.** *(Chap 6, Class-XI, New NCERT)*
1. The SHGs promote thrift in small proportions by a minimum contribution from each member.
2. From the pooled money, credit is given to the needy members to be repayable in small installments at reasonable interest rates.

Which of the statement(s) given above is/are correct?
(a) Only 1 (b) Only 2
(c) Both 1 and 2 (d) Neither 1 nor 2

↗ *Ans.* *(c)*

Exp. Both the statements (1) and (2) are correct about Self-Help Groups.
Self-Help Groups (SHGs) are informal associations of people who choose to come together to find ways for improving their living conditions. Self-Help Groups

play a prominent role in financial inclusion of rural India. They promote money pooling by small contribution by all the members to help any of the member who need help at any point of time. SHGs have emerged to fill the gap in the formal credit system.

11. **Consider the following events and arrange them in chronological order.**
(Chap 6, Class-XI, New NCERT) (UPPSC Pre 2020)
1. Establishment of NABARD
2. Self-Help Group Bank Linkage Programme
3. Kisan Credit Card Plan
4. Establishment of Regional Rural Bank

Codes
(a) 4, 1, 2, 3 (b) 4, 2, 3, 1
(c) 1, 2, 3, 4 (d) 4, 3, 2, 1

↗ *Ans.* *(a)*

Exp. The correct chronological order of events is 4, 1, 2, 3.
Regional Rural Banks (RRBs) These were established in 1975 to dispense adequate credit at cheaper rates to rural population.
NABARD National Bank for Agriculture and Rural Development was set up in 1982 as an apex body to coordinate the activities of all institutions involved in the rural financing system.
Self-Help Group Bank Linkage Programme It was started in 1992 by the NABARD to link the unorganised sector with the formal banking sector.
Kisan Credit Card Plan It was introduced in 1998 by NABARD to provide term loans to farmers for their agricultural needs.

12. **Which of the following statements about the Saansad Adarsh Gram Yojana (SAGY) is incorrect?** *(Chap 6, Class-XI, New NCERT)*
(a) Under this scheme, Members of Parliament need to identify and develop one village from their constituencies.
(b) Under this scheme, MPs have to develop one village as a model village.
(c) According to the scheme, the village can have a population of 3,000-5,000 in the plains and 1,000-3,000 in the hills and should not be MPs' own or their spouse's villages.
(d) All of the above

↗ *Ans.* *(d)*

Exp. All the given statements are incorrect about the Saansad Adarsh Gram Yojana (SAGY). This scheme was launched in October, 2014. Under this scheme, Members of Parliament (MPs) need to identify and develop one village from their constituencies. MPs have to turn these villages into model villages.

They are expected to facilitate a village development plan, motivate villagers to take up activities and built infrastructure in the areas of health, nutrition and education. The distinct feature of this yojana is that it is demand driven, inspired by society and based on people's participation.

13. **Rural credit can be classified into the following categories.** *(Chap 6, Class XI, New NCERT)*

1. Short term credit–for a period of less than 15 months.
2. Medium term credit–for a period of 3 years.
3. Long term credit–for a period of upto 5 years.

Which of the statement(s) given above is/are correct?

(a) Only 1   (b) 1 and 2
(c) 2 and 3   (d) All of these

↗ *Ans.* *(a)*

Exp. Statement (1) is correct with respect to the rural credit categories. The Indian farmers require credit to meet their short term needs viz, purchasing seeds, fertilisers, paying wages to hired workers etc. for a period of less than 15 months.

Medium term credit is a type of credit that includes credit requirements of farmers for a medium period ranging between 15 months and 5 years. Period of long term credit is more than 5 years. The purpose of long term credit is buying additional land, horticulture etc.

14. **Consider the following statements about infrastructure.** *(Chap 8, Class-XI, New NCERT)*

1. Infrastructure provides supporting services in the main areas of industrial and agricultural production, domestic and foreign trade and commerce.
2. It includes roads, railways, ports, airports, dams, power stations, oil and gas pipelines, tele-communication facilities, etc.

Which of the statement(s) given above is/are correct?

(a) Only 1   (b) Only 2
(c) Both 1 and 2   (d) Neither 1 nor 2

↗ *Ans.* *(c)*

Exp. Both the statements (1) and (2) are correct about infrastructure.

Infrastructure is the support system, which depends on the efficient working of a modern industrial economy. It provides supporting services in the main areas of industrial and agricultural production, domestic and foreign trade and commerce.

It is a catalyst which helps in enhancing the productivity of the factors of production and improving the quality of life of people.

Infrastructural services include roads, railways, ports, airports, dams, power stations, oil and gas pipelines, telecommunication facilities etc. Some of these facilities have a direct impact on production of goods and services while other give indirect support by building the social sector of economy.

15. **Consider the following statements.**
(Chap 8, Class XI, New NCERT)

1. HRIDAY was launched in 2015 with the aim of bringing together urban planning, economic growth and heritage conservation in an inclusive manner.
2. NULM was launched by the Ministry of Housing and Urban Poverty Alleviation, Government of India.

Which of the statement (s) given above is/are correct?

(a) Only 1   (b) Only 2
(c) Both 1 and 2   (d) Neither 1 nor 2

↗ *Ans.* *(c)*

Exp. Both the given statements (1) and (2) are correct. The National Heritage City Development and Augmentation Yojana (HRIDAY), a central sector scheme of the Government of India. It was launched on 21st January, 2015 with an aim of bringing together urban planning, economic growth and heritage conservation in an inclusive manner and with objective of preserving the heritage character of the city.

National Urban Livelihoods Mission (NULM) was launched by the Ministry of Housing and Urban Poverty Alleviation (MHUPA), Government of India on 23rd September, 2013 by replacing the existing Swarna Jayanti Shahari Rozgar Yojana.

06
Agriculture

New NCERT Class IX (The Story of Village Palampur), New NCERT Class IX (Food Security of India),
New NCERT Class IX (People as a Resource), New NCERT Class XI (Indian Economy 1950–1990),
New NCERT Class XI (Rural Development)

1. **Which of the following statements is incorrect regarding agriculture?** *(Chap 1, Class-IX, New NCERT)*

(a) Growing more than one crop on a piece of land during the year is known as multiple cropping.

(b) Mono cropping is the most common way of increasing production on a given piece of land.

(c) During the rainy season, farmers grow jowar and bajra.

(d) In the winter season, fields are sown with wheat.

➚ *Ans.* *(b)*

Exp. Statement (b) is incorrect regarding agriculture as multiple cropping (not mono cropping) is the most common way of increasing production on a given piece of land. To grow more than one crop on a piece of land during the year is called multiple cropping.

On the other hand, mono cropping is the practice of growing the same crop on the same piece of land, year after year.

2. **The contribution of agriculture in Indian economy is** *(Chap 2, Class-IX, New NCERT) (UPPSC Pre 2017)*

(a) increasing

(b) decreasing

(c) constant

(d) None of these

➚ *Ans.* *(b)*

Exp. The contribution of agriculture in Indian economy is decreasing as in 1947, agriculture accounted for 54% of India's GDP.

In the successive years their is a consistent decline in the contribution of agriculture into GDP. The reason being insufficient public investment for decline of agrarian development, small landholdings, lack of irrigation system etc. The contribution of agriculture sector in 1950-51 was 59% and in 1990-91 the contribution of agriculture sector was 34.9% in GDP of India. In 2018-19, the contribution of agriculture sector was 18% (approx) in GDP of India.

3. **Consider the following statements about the condition of the agriculture sector after independence.** *(Chap 4, Class-IX, New NCERT)*

1. The low productivity of the agricultural sector forced India to import food from the United States of America (USA).

2. Land ceiling fixed the minimum size of land which could be owned by an individual.

Which of the statement(s) given above is/are correct?

(a) Only 1

(b) Only 2

(c) Both 1 and 2

(d) Neither 1 nor 2

➚ *Ans.* *(a)*

Exp. Only statement (1) is correct about the condition of the agriculture sector after independence.

Due to lack of resources, primitive agriculture techniques, informal sources of credit and negligible public investment in agriculture, the total production is very low and insufficient to fullfill the needs of population. This low productivity of the agricultural sector forced India to import food from the United States of America.

Statement (2) is incorrect because land ceiling fixed the maximum (not the minimum) size of land which could be owned by the individual.

Land ceiling was the policy to promote equity in the agricultural sector. The purpose of land ceiling was to reduce the concentration of land ownership in a few hands.

4. **Consider the following statements regarding agriculture in India.** *(Chap 2, Class IX, New NCERT)*

1. Agriculture and allied sectors contribute more than 17% of Gross Domestic Product of India.
2. Share in total employment by agriculture as high as 49%.

Which of the statement(s) given above is/are correct?

(a) Only 1 (b) Only 2
(c) Both 1 and 2 (d) Neither 1 nor 2

↗ *Ans.* *(c)*

Exp. Both the statements (1) and (2) are correct regarding agriculture in India. Agriculture sector includes core farming, animal husbandry, dairy etc. Agriculture is a dominant sector in India as it contributes 17% to the total Gross Domestic Product (GDP). It plays an important role in the Indian economy as around 49% of the population is still dependent on agriculture and allied activities.

5. **Which of the following statements is correct regarding agricultural yield?**

(Chap 1, Class-IX, New NCERT)

(a) Yield is measured as crop produced on a given piece of land during a full year.
(b) Till the mid-1960s, the seeds used in cultivation were traditional ones with relatively low yields.
(c) Traditional seeds needed more irrigation.
(d) All of the above

↗ *Ans.* *(b)*

Exp. Statement (b) is correct regarding agricultural yield. Till the mid-1960s, the seeds used in cultivation were traditional ones with relatively low yields. High Yielding Varieties (HYV) of seeds introduced during Green Revolution, contributed in producing greater amounts of grain on a same crop.

As a result, the same piece of land would now produce larger quantities of foodgrains that was possible earlier.

Statements (a) and (c) are incorrect because yield is measured as crop produced on a given piece of land during a single season. Traditional seeds needed less irrigation as farmers use cow dung and other traditional manure as fertilisers in their cultivation.

6. **Consider the following statements.**

(Chap 2, Class-IX, New NCERT)

1. The Green Revolution in the late 1960s introduced the Indian farmer to cultivation of wheat and rice using HYV seeds.
2. HYV seeds needed plenty of water, chemical fertilisers and pesticides to produce best results.

Which of the statements given above is/are incorrect?

(a) Only 1 (b) Only 2
(c) Both 1 and 2 (d) Neither 1 nor 2

↗ *Ans.* *(d)*

Exp. Neither statement (1) nor (2) is incorrect.

The Green Revolution in late 1960s introduced the Indian farmers to cultivation of wheat and rice using HYV seeds. In comparison to the traditional seeds, the HYV seeds promised to produce much greater amounts of grain on a single plant.

HYV seeds needed plenty of water, chemical fertilisers and pesticides to produce best results. Thus, higher yields were possible only from a combination of HYV seeds, better irrigation, chemical fertilisers, pesticides etc.

7. **Which of the following areas did not witness the first phase of the Green Revolution?**

(Chap 1, Class-IX, New NCERT)

(a) Haryana (b) Madhya Pradesh
(c) Western Uttar Pradesh (d) Punjab

↗ *Ans.* *(b)*

Exp. Madhya Pradesh did not witness the first phase of the Green Revolution introduced in late 1960s. Farmers of Haryana, Punjab and Western Uttar Pradesh were benefitted a lot in the first phase of the Green Revolution.

The farmers in these regions set up tube wells for irrigation and made use of HYV seeds, chemical fertilisers and pesticides in farming. Some of them bought farm machinery like tractors and thrashers, which made ploughing and harvesting faster, and were rewarded with high yields.

8. **Which one of the following most appropriately describes the nature of Green Revolution of late sixties of 20th century?** *(Chap 2, Class XI, New NCERT)*

(BPSC Pre 2018)

(a) Intensive cultivation of green vegetables
(b) Intensive Agriculture District Programme
(c) High Yielding Varieties Programme
(d) Seed-Fertiliser-Water Technology

↗ *Ans.* *(d)*

Exp. Among the given options, Seed-Fertiliser-Water technology most appropriately describes the nature of Green Revolution of late sixties of 20th century.

Green Revolution can be defined as seed-water -fertilisers, because the combination of all three leads to the mass production in agriculture.

High Yielding Variety of seeds, new irrigation techniques and more irrigation system were used along with the use of fertilisers to gain the benefits of Green Revolution.

This revolution was pioneered by the Indian Government in mid 1960s upto mid 1970s but the use of HYV seed was restricted to more affluent states such as Punjab, Andhra Pradesh and Tamil Nadu.

9. The Green Revolution in India has contributed to
(Chap 2, Class-XI, New NCERT) (WBPSC Pre 2007)

(a) inter-regional inequality
(b) inter-class inequality
(c) inter-crop inequality
(d) All of these

↗ *Ans.* (d)

Exp. The Green Revolution in India has contributed to inter-regional, inter-class and inter-crop inequality. In context of regions (states), it was initiated and successful in the regions such as Haryana, Punjab and Western Uttar Pradesh whereas other states were left behind lead to inter-regional inequality.

It also favoured the rich peasants having large holdings and gave preference to cultivation of rice and wheat over coarse grains which lead to the growth in inter-class inequality and preference of growing wheat and rice over other coarse grains that lead to unequal crop productions with regard to consumption.

10. Which of the following statements is incorrect regarding the effects of the Green Revolution?
(Chap 1, Class-IX, New NCERT)

(a) Scientific reports indicate that the Green Revolution has overused the natural resource base.
(b) In many areas, Green Revolution is associated with the loss of soil fertility due to increased use of chemical fertilisers.
(c) Continuous use of groundwater for tubewell irrigation has led to the depletion of the water-table.
(d) None of the above

↗ *Ans.* (d)

Exp. None of the given statements is incorrect regarding the effects of the Green Revolution.

It is necessary to use land carefully as it is a natural resource. Scientific reports indicate that the modern farming methods have overused the natural resource base.

In many areas, Green Revolution resulted into loss of soil fertility due to increased use of chemical fertilisers. Chemical fertilisers provide minerals which dissolve in water and immediately available to plants. But these may not be retained in soil for long and may escape from soil and pollute groundwater, rivers and lakes. Chemical fertilisers can also kill bacteria and micro-organisms in soil and result into loss of soil fertility.

Continuous use of groundwater for tubewell irrigation has also led to the depletion of water-table.

11. With reference to the use of chemical fertilisers in Indian agriculture, which of the given statement(s) is/are correct?
(Chap 1, Class-IX, New NCERT)

1. Punjab is the largest consumer of chemical fertilisers in India.
2. A substantial amount of fertiliser subsidy also benefits the fertiliser industry.

Codes
(a) Only 1
(b) Only 2
(c) Both 1 and 2
(d) Neither 1 nor 2

↗ *Ans.* (c)

Exp. Both the statements (1) and (2) are correct regarding the use of chemical fertilisers in Indian agriculture. The Green Revolution first initiated in Punjab encouraged farmers besides using HYV seeds to use chemical fertilisers on extensive scale. However, with declining productivity, farmers in Punjab were compelled to use more chemical fertilisers to sustain productivity of land, this has increased the cost of production.

In India, fertiliser subsidy is granted to fertiliser industry which in turn is responsible for passing it to farmers. However, due to discrepancies present in this mechanism, a substantial amount of fertiliser subsidy also benefits the fertiliser industry.

12. Which of the following is not a parameter of food security?
(Chap 4, Class-IX, New NCERT)

(a) Accessibility
(b) Affordability
(c) Availability
(d) Adaptability

↗ *Ans.* (d)

Exp. Adaptability is not a parameter of food security. Food security means availability, accessibility and affordability of food to all people at all times.

Availability of food means sufficient reserves of food within the country. Accessibility means food is within reach of every person. Affordability implies that an individual has enough money to buy sufficient, safe and nutritious food to meet ones dietary needs.

13. Consider the following statements with respect to famine.
(Chap 4, Class-IX, New NCERT)

1. A famine is widespread scarcity of food, caused by several factors including war, natural disasters, crop failure etc.
2. The most devastating famine that occurred in India was the Famine of Bengal in 1943.

Which of the statement(s) given above is/are correct?

(a) Only 1
(b) Only 2
(c) Both 1 and 2
(d) Neither 1 nor 2

↗ *Ans.* (c)

Exp. Both the statements (1) and (2) are correct with respect to famine.

A famine is a condition of scarcity of food in which deaths are caused due to hunger. This situation can be caused by many reasons such as a war, natural disaster, crop failure, drought, pandemic etc.

The most devastating famine that occurred in India was the Famine of Bengal in 1943. This famine killed around thirty lakh people in the province of Bengal. The agricultural labourers, fisherman, transport workers, etc were most adversely affected by this famine.

14. Consider the following Assertion (A) and Reason (R) and choose the correct code.

(Chap 4, Class-IX, New NCERT)

Assertion (A) The rising Minimum Support Prices (MSP) have raised the maintenance cost of procuring food grains for the government.

Reason (R) Rising transportation and storage costs of the FCI are other contributing factors in this increase.

Codes

(a) Both A and R are true and R is the correct explanation of A.

(b) Both A and R are true, but R is not the correct explanation of A.

(c) A is true, but R is false.

(d) A is false, but R is true.

↗ *Ans.* (b)

Exp. Both Assertion (A) and Reason (R) are true but Reason (R) is not the correct explanation of Assertion (A).

The rising Minimum Support Price (MSP) have raised the maintenance cost of procuring food grains for the government. The increased food grains procurement at enhanced MSP is the result of the pressure exerted by leading foodgrain producing states such as Punjab, Haryana, Andhra Pradesh etc.

Rising transportation and storage costs of the Food Corporation of India (FCI) are other contributing factors in this increase. The storage of massive food stocks has been responsible for high carrying costs, in addition to wastage and deterioration in grain quality.

15. Who among the following released a 'Wheat Revolution stamp' in July 1968 to commemorate Green Revolution in India?

(Chap 4, Class-IX, New NCERT)

(a) Morarji Desai   (b) MS Swaminathan

(c) Indira Gandhi   (d) None of these

↗ *Ans.* (c)

Exp. Indira Gandhi, the then Prime Minister of India officially recorded the impressive strides of Green Revolution in agriculture by releasing a 'Wheat Revolution stamp' in July 1968. It is because after the introduction of Green Revolution, India got self-sufficiency in foodgrains, which was aimed since independence.

Green Revolution not only led towards self-sufficiency in foodgrains but also in reduction of seasonal as well as chronic hunger.

16. Consider the following statements about buffer stock. *(Chap 4, Class-IX, New NCERT)*

1. Buffer Stock is the stock of foodgrains, namely wheat and jowar, procured by the government through the FCI.

2. The FCI purchases wheat and rice from the farmers in states where there is surplus production.

Which of the statement(s) given above is/are incorrect?

(a) Only 1   (b) Only 2

(c) Both 1 and 2   (d) Neither 1 nor 2

↗ *Ans.* (a)

Exp. Statement (1) is incorrect about buffer stock as it is the stock of foodgrains, namely wheat and rice (not jowar), procured by government through Food Corporation of India (FCI).

Statement (2) is correct. In buffer stock, the FCI purchases wheat and rice from the farmers in states where there is surplus production.

A buffer stock is maintained to distribute the procured food grain in the food-deficit areas and for the poors through ration shops. It is also maintained to deal with any unprecedented situation like crop failure.

17. Which of the following statements is incorrect regarding agriculture allied sector?

(Chap 4, Class IX, New NCERT)

(a) India is the largest producer of milk in the world.

(b) India is the fourth largest fish producing nation in the world.

(c) Floriculture is a branch of horticulture.

(d) India is home to more than 10% of the global fish diversity.

↗ *Ans.* (b)

Exp. Statement (b) is incorrect regarding agriculture allied sector. Presently, India is the second largest aquaculture nation in the world. The Indian fisheries sector is sunrise sector.

18. **Who determines the Minimum Support Price in India?** *(Chap 4, Class-IX, New NCERT) (BPSC Pre 2019)*

(a) Commission for Agricultural Costs and Prices
(b) Ministry of Agriculture and Farmer's Welfare
(c) Finance Commission
(d) NABARD

↗ *Ans. (a)*

Exp. The Commission for Agricultural Costs and Prices determines the Minimum Support Price (MSP) in India. Final decision regarding MSP is taken by Union Cabinet headed by Prime Minister. It is declared by the government every year before the sowing season to provide incentives to farmers for raising the production of these crops.

19. **The price at which the government purchases foodgrains for maintaining the Public Distribution System (PDS) and for building up buffer stocks is known as**
(Chap 4, Class-IX, New NCERT) (IAS Pre 2001)

(a) Minimum Support Price   (b) Procurement Price
(c) Issue Price   (d) Ceiling Price

↗ *Ans. (b)*

Exp. The price at which the government purchases foodgrains for maintaining the Public Distribution System (PDS) and for building up buffer stocks is known as procurement price. This price is lower than the market price.

Procurement price is declared after harvesting of crops. The procurement agencies step in to procure the crop and support the price when the market price falls below the MSP and the procured farm products are kept in government warehouses and distributed through the PDS.

20. **Consider the following statements.**
(Chap 4, Class-IX, New NCERT)

1. Subsidy is a payment that a government makes to a producer to supplement the market price of a commodity.
2. Subsidies can keep consumer prices high while maintaining a higher income for domestic producers.

Which of the statement(s) given above is/are correct?

(a) Only 1   (b) Only 2
(c) Both 1 and 2   (d) Neither 1 nor 2

↗ *Ans. (a)*

Exp. Statement (1) is correct as subsidy is a payment that a government makes to a producer to supplement the market price of a commodity.

It leads to a fall in the price of the subsidised product. The objective of subsidy is to encourage the welfare of the society.

Statement (2) is incorrect because subsidies can keep consumer prices low (not high) while maintaining a higher income for domestic producers by increasing compitativeness of the product.

21. **Academy of Development Science (ADS) has facilitated a network of NGOs for setting up grain banks in different regions in which of the following states?** *(Chap 4, Class-IX, New NCERT)*

(a) Haryana   (b) Maharashtra
(c) Uttar Pradesh   (d) Punjab

↗ *Ans. (b)*

Exp. Academy of Development Science (ADS) has facilitated a network of NGOs for setting up grain banks in different regions in Maharashtra. It organises training and capacity building programmes on food security for NGOs. ADS efforts to set up grain banks, to facilitate replication through other NGOs and to influence the Government's policy on Food Security, are thus paying rich dividend.

22. **……… is a process that involves the assembling, storage, processing, transportation, packaging, grading and distribution of different agricultural commodities across the country.**
(Chap 4, Class-IX, New NCERT)

(a) Agricultural marketing   (b) Food processing
(c) Agricultural rationing   (d) None of these

↗ *Ans. (a)*

Exp. Agricultural marketing is a process that involves the assembling, storage, processing, transportation, packaging, grading and distribution of different agricultural commodities across the country. Prior to independence, farmers while selling their produce to traders suffered from faulty weighing, manipulation of accounts, lack of information on prices prevailing in markets.

They also did not have proper storage facilities and they used to sell their produce at lower prices. For overcoming these problems, Agricultural Marketing System came into existence.

23. **Consider the following Assertion (A) and Reason (R) and choose the correct code.**
(Chap 2, Class-XI, New NCERT)

Assertion (A) Fertiliser and pesticide subsidies result in overuse of resources which can be harmful to the environment.

Reason (R) Subsidies provide an incentive for wasteful use of resources.

Codes

(a) Both A and R are true and R is the correct explanation of A.

(b) Both A and R are true, but R is not the correct explanation of A.

(c) A is true, but R is false.

(d) A is false, but R is true.

↗ *Ans.* *(a)*

Exp. Both Assertion (A) and Reason (R) are true and Reason (R) is the correct explanation of Assertion (A).

Fertiliser and pesticide subsidies were given by the government to provide an incentive for adoption of new HYV technology by farmers. Therefore, subsidies were needed to encourage farmers to test the new technology.

However, fertilisers and pesticides subsidies result in overuse of resources which can be harmful to the environment. Chemical fertilisers pollute the environment as well as reduce soil fertility.

Subsidies provide an incentive for overuse, which lead to wasteful use of resources.

24. **Which of the following is not one of the measures taken for agricultural marketing?**

(Chap 6, Class-XI, New NCERT)

(a) Regulation of markets to create orderly and transparent marketing conditions.

(b) Provision of physical infrastructure facilities like roads, railways, warehouses, godowns, cold storages and processing units.

(c) Minor forest produce collection.

(d) Minimum Support Price.

↗ *Ans.* *(c)*

Exp. Minor forest produce collection is not one of the measures taken for agricultural marketing.

Following are the four measures that were initiated to improve the marketing aspect

- The first step was regulation of markets to create orderly and transparent marketing conditions.
- The second component is the provision of physical infrastructure facilities, such as roads, railways, warehouses, godowns, cold storage etc.
- The third aspect of government initiative is cooperative marketing in realising fair prices for farmers' products.
- The fourth element is the policy instruments including
  - Assurance of Minimum Support Price
  - Maintenance of buffer stocks of wheat and rice by Food Corporation of India
  - Distribution of foodgrain and sugar through Public Distribution System

25. **Which of the following factors/policies were affecting the price of rice in India in the recent past?** *(Chap 4, Class-IX, New NCERT) (IAS Pre 2020)*

1. Minimum Support Price
2. Government's trading
3. Government's stockpiling
4. Consumer subsidies

Codes

(a) 1, 2 and 4   (b) 1, 3 and 4

(c) 2 and 3   (d) 1, 2, 3 and 4

↗ *Ans.* *(d)*

Exp. All of the given factors/policies were affecting the price of rice in India in the recent past. The Minimum Support Price and consumer subsidies through Public Distribution System (PDS) tend to artificially increase or decrease the price of rice.

Similarly, Government's trading and stockpiling tend to inflate the price of rice regardless of its condition of demand and supply.

Subsidies given by government through various food distribution schemes impact the price in the market directly or indirectly.

26. **Consider the following statements.**

(Chap 4, Class IX, New NCERT)

1. Pradhan Mantri Fasal Bima Yojana replaced the MNAIS and NAIS.
2. PM<-KISAN is being implemented by the Ministry of Agriculture and farmers welfare.

Which of the statement(s) given above is/are correct?

(a) Only 1   (b) Only 2

(c) Both 1 and 2   (d) Neither 1 nor 2

↗ *Ans.* *(c)*

Exp. Both the statements (1) and (2) are correct. Pradhan Mantri Fasal Bima Yojana (PMFBY) was launched in 2016. It replaced the National Agricultural Insurance Scheme (NAIS) and Modified National Agricultural Insurance Scheme (MNAIS). It aims to provide a comprehensive insurance cover against the failure of the crop thus helping in stabilising the income of the farmers.

Pradhan Mantri Kisan Samman Nidhi (PM-KISAN) was launched in February 2019. It is a Central Sector scheme. It is being implemented by the Ministry of Agriculture and Farmers' Welfare. Under the scheme, the Central government transfers an amount of ₹ 6,000 per year, in 3 equal installments, directly into the bank accounts of all landholding farmers irrespective of the size of their landholdings.

27. Consider the following statements.

(Chap 6, Class XI, New NCERT)

1. TRIFED is a national level apex organisation functioning under the administrative control of the Ministry of Tribal Affairs.
2. The AGMARKNET is a G2C e-governance portal.
3. ICAR is headquartered at Mumbai.
4. FAO is one of the UN Food Aid Organisations based in Rome (Italy).

Which of the statement(s) given above is/are correct?

(a) 1, 2 and 3   (b) 1, 2 and 4
(c) 2, 3 and 4   (d) 1, 2, 3 and 4

➢ *Ans.* (b)

Exp. Statements (1), (2) and (4) are correct. Tribal Cooperative Marketing Development Federation of India (TRIFED) came into existence in 1987. It is a National level apex organisation functioning under the Ministry of Tribal Affairs. Its head office is located in New Delhi.

The AGMARKNET is a Government to Citizen (G2C) e-governance portal. It caters to the needs of various Stakeholders such as farmers, industry, policy makers and academic institutions by providing agricultural marketing related information from a single window.

Food and Agriculture Organisation (FAO) is a specialised agency of the United Nation. It is one of the UN food aid organisations based in Rome (Italy). The Indian Council for Agricultural Research (ICAR) was established on 16th July, 1929. It is headquartered at New Delhi.

28. Consider the following statements regarding horticulture.

(Chap 6, Class-XI, New NCERT)

1. The Horticulture sector contributes nearly one-third of the value of agricultural output and 6% of Gross Domestic Product of India.
2. Flower harvesting, nursery maintenance, hybrid seed production and tissue culture, propagation of fruits, flowers and food processing are covered under Horticulture sector.

Which of the statement(s) given above is/are correct?

(a) Only 1   (b) Only 2
(c) Both 1 and 2   (d) Neither 1 nor 2

➢ *Ans.* (c)

Exp. Both the statements (1) and (2) are correct regarding horticulture.

Horticulture sector contributes nearly one-third of the value of agricultural output and 6% of GDP of India.

India has emerged as a world leader in producing variety of fruits like mangoes, bananas, coconuts, cashew nuts and a number of spices. It is also the second largest producer of fruits and vegetables.

Flowers harvesting, nursery maintenance, hybrid seed production and tissue culture, propagation of fruits, flowers and food processing are covered under Horticulture sector. Horticulture sector not only play a vital role in providing food and nutrition but also address the employment concern.

29. ....is known as a system of farming that restores, maintains and enhances the ecological balance.

(Chap 6, Class-XI, New NCERT)

(a) Tissue agriculture   (b) Organic agriculture
(c) Terrace farming   (d) Monoculture

➢ *Ans.* (b)

Exp. Organic agriculture is known as a system of farming that restores, maintains and enhances the ecological balance.

Many countries have around 10% of their food system under organic farming. Organic agriculture offers a means to substitute costlier agricultural inputs with locally produced organic inputs that are cheaper and thereby generate good returns on investment. It also generates income through export due to its higher demand in market. Organic Products are pesticide free and produced in an environmentally sustainable way.

30. Which of the following statements is/are correct?

(Chap 6, Class XI, New NCERT)

(a) Sikkim became the first state in the world to be fully organic in 2016.
(b) Mission Organic Value Chain Development for North-East region is a sub-mission under NMSA.
(c) Under PKVY, organic farming is promoted through adoption of organic villages by cluster approach.
(d) All of the above

➢ *Ans.* (d)

Exp. All the statement (a), (b) and (c) are correct. Sikkim became the first state in the world to be fully organic in 2016. North-East India has traditionally been organic and the consumption of chemical is far less than the rest of the country.

Mission Organic Value Chain Development for North-East Region (MOVCD-NER) is a central sector scheme, a sub-mission under National Mission for Sustainable Agriculture (NMSA). Paramparagat Krishi Vikas Yojana (PKVY) was launched in 2015. Under PKVY, organic farming is promoted through adoption of organic village by cluster approach and Participatory Guarantee System (PGS) Certification.

07

Industry

Old NCERT Class IX & X (Towards Economic Development), Old NCERT Class IX & X (The State and Economic Development), New NCERT Class XI (Indian Economy on the Eve of Independence), New NCERT Class XI (Indian Economy 1950–1990), New NCERT Class XI (Liberalisation, Privatisation and Globalisation : An Appraisal)

1. **Which type of industry can produce machine tools, which in turn are used for producing articles for current consumption?**

(Chap 1, Class-XI, New NCERT)

(a) Consumer Goods Industries
(b) Capital Goods Industries
(c) Giffen Goods Industries
(d) None of the above

↗ **Ans.** *(b)*

Exp. Industries, which can produce machine tools which are in turn, used for producing articles for current consumption are known as capital goods industries. Capital goods industries manufacture product and services that consumers will use on later.

All durable goods like cars, trucks, refrigerators, buildings, air crafts, air fields and submarine that are used to provide goods and services for sale in the market are part of capital goods.

2. **A labour intensive industry is the one that**

(Chap 4, Class-IX & X, Old NCERT) (UPPSC Pre 2006)

(a) requires hard manual labour.
(b) pays adequate wages to the labour.
(c) employs more hands.
(d) provides facilities to labour.

↗ **Ans.** *(c)*

Exp. A labour intensive industry is one that employs more hands. These types of industries provide employment to the large number of people. They are generally found in developing countries where availability of semi-skilled workforce is high. Bidi industry, bangle industry, textile industry are examples of labour intensive industries.

3. **Consider the following statements about the Industrial policy of India?** *(Chap-3 Class XI, New NCERT)*

1. Industrial Policy Resolution of 1948 classified industries of India into 15 broad areas.
2. Industrial Policy of 1956 provided the basic framework for the government's policy in regard to industries till June 1990.

Which of the statement(s) given above is/are incorrect?

(a) Only 1
(b) Only 2
(c) Both 1 and 2
(d) Neither 1 nor 2

↗ **Ans.** *(c)*

Exp. Both the statements (1) and (2) are incorrect about the Industrial Policy of India. The Industrial Policy Resolution, 1948 is the first industrial policy announced in April 1948. Industries classified into four categories viz, Public sector, Mixed sector, Controlled private sector and Private and Cooperative sector. Industrial Policy of 1956 provided the basic framework for the government's policy in regard to industries till June 1991. Industrial Policy of 1956 was regarded as the Economic Constitution of India or the Bible of State Capitalism.

4. **Consider the following statements regarding small scale industries.** *(Chap 2, Class-XI, New NCERT)*

1. A 'Small-scale industry' is defined with reference to the maximum investment allowed on the assets of a unit.
2. At present, the maximum investment allowed is ₹ 5 crores.

Which of the statement(s) given above is/are correct?

(a) Only 1
(b) Only 2
(c) Both 1 and 2
(d) Neither 1 nor 2

↗ *Ans.* (a)

Exp. Statement (1) is correct regarding small scale industries. A 'small scale industry' is defined with reference to the maximum investment allowed on the assets of a unit. This limit has changed over a period of time. In 1950, a small scale industrial unit was one which invested a maximum of ₹ 5 lakh.

As per new definition, small scale industrial unit is one with an investment of not more than ₹ 10 crore and a turnover of ₹ 50 crore. It is believed that small scale industries are more 'labour intensive' i.e. they use more labour than the large scale industries and therefore, generate more employment.

5. **Which of the following was the basis of the Industrial Licensing System in India?**

(Chap 5, Class-IX & X, Old NCERT)

(a) Industrial Development and Regulation Act, 1951
(b) Industrial Policy Resolution, 1956
(c) Industrial Policy Resolution, 1948
(d) None of the above

↗ *Ans.* (a)

Exp. Industrial Development and Regulation Act, 1951 was the basis of Industrial Licensing System in India. Under this Act, every Industrial establishment except those operated by Central Government, needed to obtain license. This Act aimed to regulate the pattern and direction of industrial development. However, it led to monopoly and curbed competition.

6. **Which one of the following industrial policies has abolished (with a few exceptions) the industrial licensing?**

(Chap 5, Class-IX & X, Old NCERT) *(WBPSC Pre 2008)*

(a) Industrial Policy, 1970   (b) Industrial Policy, 1980
(c) Industrial Policy, 1991   (d) Industrial Policy, 1985

↗ *Ans.* (c)

Exp. The Industrial Policy, 1991 has abolished the industrial licensing. This reform was introduced as a part of Liberalisation, Privatisation and Globalisation (LPG) measure introduced in 1991. The Industrial Licensing System introduced through Industrial Development and Regulation Act, 1951 restricted the growth of industries in India.

7. **Consider the following Assertion (A) and Reason (R) and choose the correct code.**

(Chap 2, Class-XI, New NCERT)

Assertion (A) The excessive regulation of industries came to be called as the License Permit Raj, prevented certain firms from becoming more efficient.

Reason (R) More time was spent by industrialists in trying to obtain a license or lobby with the concerned ministries rather than on thinking about how to improve their products.

Codes

(a) Both A and R are true and R is the correct explanation of A.
(b) Both A and R are true, but R is not the correct explanation of A.
(c) A is true, but R is false.
(d) A is false, but R is true.

↗ *Ans.* (a)

Exp. Both Assertion (A) and Reason (R) are true and Reason (R) is the correct explanation of Assertion (A).

The excessive regulation of industries came to be called as the License Permit Raj, prevented certain firms from becoming more efficient.

It is because the need to obtain a license to start an industry was misused by industrial houses. A big industrialists would get license not for starting a new firm but to prevent competitors from starting new firms.

More time was spent by industrialists in trying to obtain a license or lobby with the concerned ministries rather than on thinking about how to improve their products.

8. **Which of the following crisis led to the introduction of the New Economic Policy in 1991?** *(Chap 3, Class-XI, New NCERT)*

(a) Banking Liquidity Crisis
(b) Foreign Investment Crisis
(c) Foreign Exchange Crisis
(d) None of the above

↗ *Ans.* (c)

Exp. Foreign Exchange Crisis led to the introduction of the New Economic Policy in 1991. In 1991, India met with an economic crisis relating to its external debt.

The Government was not able to make repayments on its borrowing from abroad. During that time, foreign exchange borrowed from other countries and International Financial Institutions was spent on meeting consumption needs.

Foreign exchange reserve, that we generally maintain to import petroleum and other items dropped to level that were not sufficient for even a fortnight. All these led the government to introduce a new set of policy measures which changed the direction of our developmental strategies in 1991.

9. Which among the following statements is incorrect regarding the New Economic Policy (NEP) of 1991? *(Chap 3, Class-XI, New NCERT)*

(a) The thrust of the policy was towards creating a more competitive environment in the economy and removing the barriers to entry and growth of firms.

(b) The set of policies can broadly be classified into two groups i.e. the stabilisation measures and the structural reform measures.

(c) Stabilisation measures are long-term measures, intended to correct some of the weaknesses that have developed in the balance of payments and to bring inflation under control.

(d) None of the above

➚ *Ans.* (c)

Exp. Statement (c) is incorrect regarding the New Economic Policy (NEP) of 1991 as stabilisation measures were short-term measures, intended to correct some of the weaknesses that have developed in the balance of payments and to bring inflation under control. In simple words, this means that there was a need to maintain sufficient foreign exchange reserves and keep the rising price under control.

10. Consider the following statements about deregulation of the industrial sector.

(Chap 3, Class-XI, New NCERT)

1. Industrial licensing was abolished for almost all except alcohols, cigarettes, hazardous chemicals, industrial explosives, electronics, aerospace, drugs and pharmaceuticals.

2. The only industries which are now reserved for the public sector are a part of atomic energy generation and some core activities in railway transport.

Which of the statement(s) given above is/are incorrect?

(a) Only 1   (b) Only 2

(c) Both 1 and 2   (d) Neither 1 nor 2

➚ *Ans.* (d)

Exp. Neither statement (1) nor (2) is incorrect about deregulation of the industrial sector.

The reform policies introduced in and after 1991 removed many of the trade restrictions.

Industrial licensing was abolished for almost all but for product categories like alcohols, cigarettes, hazardous chemicals, industrial explosives, electronics, aerospace, drugs and pharmaceuticals.

The only industries which are now reserved for public sector are a part of atomic energy generation and some core activities in railway transport.

11. Consider the following statements.

(Chap-3, Class XI, New NCERT)

1. There are a total of 10 maharatna companies in India.

2. MSMEs is the second largest employment generating sector after agriculture.

Which of statement(s) given above is/are correct?

(a) Only 1   (b) Only 2

(c) Both 1 and 2   (d) Neither 1 nor 2

➚ *Ans.* (c)

Exp. Both the statements (1) and (2) are correct. There are a total of 10 maharatna companies in India. These are

- Bharat Heavy Electricals Limited (BHEL)
- Bharat Petroleum Corporation Limited (BPCL)
- Coal India Limited (CIL)
- Gas Authority of India Limited (GAIL)
- Hindustan Petroleum Corporation Limited (HPCL)
- Indian Oil Corporation Limited (IOCL)
- National Thermal Power Corporation Limited (NTPC)
- Oil and Natural Gas Corporation Limited (ONGC)
- Power Grid Corporation of India Limited (PGCIL)
- Steel Authority of India Limited (SAIL)

Micro, Small and Medium Enterprises (MSME) is the second largest employment generating sector after agriculture. It provides employment to around 120 million people in India.

12. Which of the following industries fall under the purview of industrial licensing that requires compulsory licensing? *(Chap 3, Class XI, New NCERT)*

1. Industrial explosive
2. Hazardous chemicals
3. Cigars and cigarettes of tobacco
4. Animal fats and oil

Codes

(a) 1, 2 and 4   (b) 1, 2 and 3

(c) 2, 3 and 4   (d) 1, 2, 3 and 4

➚ *Ans.* (b)

Exp. Statements (1), (2) and (3) fall under the purview of industrial licensing that require compulsory licensing. There are only 4 industries at present related to security, strategic and environmental concerns, where an industrial licence is currently required. These are

- Electronic aerospace and defiance equipment.
- Specified hazardous chemicals.
- Industrial explosives.
- Cigars and cigarettes of tobacco and manufactured tobacco substitutes.

13. In the 'Index of core industries', which one of the following is given the highest weight overlapping? *(Chap 3, Class-XI, New NCERT) (IAS Pre 2015)*

(a) Coal Production   (b) Electricity Generation
(c) Fertilisers Production   (d) Steel Production

↗ *Ans.* *(b)*

Exp. The 8 core industries in India in decreasing order of their weightage are

Refinery Products > Electricity Generation Steel Production > Coal > Crude oil > Natural Gas > Cement > Fertilisers production.

These industries comprise 40.27% of the weight of item included in the Index of Industrial Production.

14. Consider the following objectives of the Trade Reforms after 1991. *(Chap 3, Class-XI, New NCERT)*

1. Dismantling of qualitative restrictions on imports and exports.
2. Reduction of tariff rates.
3. Removal of licensing procedures for imports.

Which of the statement(s) given above is/are incorrect?

(a) Only 1   (b) Only 2   (c) 1, 2 and 3   (d) 1 and 3

↗ *Ans.* *(a)*

Exp. Statement (1) is incorrect regarding the objectives of the Trade Policy Reforms after 1991. The Trade Reforms after 1991 aimed at as dismantling of quantitative (not qualitative) restrictions on imports and exports.

Trade and Investment Policy Reforms were introduced to promote the efficiency of local industries and adoption of modern technologies.

In the light of trade policy reforms, import licensing was abolished and also export duties were removed.

15. Which of the following industry classifications and their examples are incorrectly matched?

(Chap 3, Class-XI, New NCERT)

(a) Maharatna   – Steel Authority of India Limited
(b) Navratna   – Bharat Sanchar Nigam Limited
(c) Miniratna   – Mahanagar Telephone Nigam Limited
(d) Both 'b' and 'c'

↗ *Ans.* *(d)*

Exp. Pairs (b) and (c) are incorrectly matched.
Bharat Sanchar Nigam Limited (BSNL) comes under 'Miniratna' while Mahanagar Telephone Nigam Limited (MTNL) is a 'Navratna' company.

In order to improve efficiency, infuse professionalism and enable them to compete more effectively in the liberalised global environment, the government identifies PSEs and declare them as Maharatna, Navratnas and Miniratnas.

They are given greater managerial and operational autonomy to run the company efficiently and increase their profits.

16. Which of the following has led to the slowdown in growth of the industrial Sector?

(Chap 4, Class-IX & X, Old NCERT)

(a) Availability of cheaper exports
(b) More Foreign Investment
(c) Availability of cheaper imports
(d) All of the above

↗ *Ans.* *(c)*

Exp. Availability of cheaper imports has led to the slowdown in growth of the industrial sector.

In a globalised world, developing countries are compelled to open up their economies to greater flow of goods and capital from developed countries and rendering their industries vulnerable to imported goods.

Cheaper import has thus, replaced the demand for domestic goods as the domestic manufacturers are facing competition from imports.

17. Consider the following statements.

(Chap 4, Class-IX & X, Old NCERT)

1. MUDRA was launched by the government in 2015 for providing loans up to ₹ 10 lakh.
2. The programme Make in India started in September 2014.
3. AIM-iCREST programme launched by NITI Aayog.

Which of the statement(s) given above is/are correct?

(a) 1 and 2   (b) 1, 2 and 3
(c) 2 and 3   (d) None of these

↗ *Ans.* *(b)*

Exp. All the statements (1), (2) and (3) are correct. MUDRA is financial institution set up by the Government of India in 2015 for providing loan upto ₹ 10 lakh to the non-corporate, non-farms small-micro-enterprises.

The Make in India Campaign was launched by the Prime Minister of India on 25th September, 2014. Make in India Campaign aims at reviving the job creative manufacturing sector, which is being seen as the key to take the Indian economy on a sustainable high growth rate. AIM-iCREST launched by Atal Innovation Mission is an Incubator Capabilities Enhancement Programme launched by NITI Aayog for a Robust Ecosystem focused on creating high performing startups.

08

Money and Banking

Old NCERT Class IX & X (The Infrastructure of the Indian Economy), Old NCERT Class IX & X (The State and Economic Development), New NCERT Class X (Money and Credit), New NCERT Class XII (Money and Banking), Old NCERT Class XII (Money and Banking System Appendix)

1. Consider the following statements regarding the barter system. *(Chap 3, Class-IX & X, Old NCERT)*

1. Economic exchanges without the mediation of money are referred to as barter exchanges.
2. 'Double coincidence of wants' is absent in barter system.

Which of the statement(s) given above is/are incorrect?

(a) Only 1   (b) Only 2
(c) Both 1 and 2   (d) Neither 1 nor 2

↗ *Ans.* (b)

Exp. Statement (2) is incorrect regarding the barter system because barter system presumes the 'double coincidence of wants'.

It means for the completion of barter, both parties, the seller and buyers have to agree to sell and buy commodities from each other. There is no need of the mediation of money in barter exchange.

2. With reference to 'function of money', which of the following statements are correct?

(Chap 3, Class-XII, New NCERT)

1. It acts as a medium of exchange.
2. It acts as a convenient unit of account.
3. It acts as a store of value.

Codes

(a) 1 and 2   (b) 2 and 3
(c) 1 and 3   (d) 1, 2 and 3

↗ *Ans.* (d)

Exp. All the given statements (1), (2) and (3) are correct regarding 'function of money'.

Money is the most liquid of all assets and is universally accepted, so it is used as a medium of exchange.

The value of all goods and services can be expressed in monetary units hence, it also serves as a convenient unit of account. Further, money is not perishable and its storage cost is considerably lower. Thus, it can also act as a store of value for individuals.

3. Which of the following statements is correct about the currency issued by the government?

(Chap 7, Class-XII, Old NCERT)

(a) ₹ 100 is a legal tender.
(b) The legal tender of coins of value 50 paise and ₹ 1 is limited.
(c) All of the above
(d) None of the above

↗ *Ans.* (b)

Exp. Both the statements (a) and (b) are correct. The currency issued by the government. (₹ 1, ₹ 5, ₹ 10, ₹ 20, ₹ 50, ₹ 100, ₹ 200, ₹ 500, ₹ 2000) are called legal tenders, as they cannot be refused by any citizen of the country for settlement of any kind of transaction.

Currency and notes do not have intrinsic value like gold or silver but they derive the value from the guarantee provided by the issuing authority of these items.

The legal tender of coins of value 50 paise and ₹ 1 is limited. Coin of any denomination not lower than ₹ 1 shall be legal tender for any sum not exceeding ₹ 1000 on the other hand, 50 paise coins shall be legal tender for any sum not exceeding ₹ 10.

4. Which of the following schemes of the Government of India focusses on a cashless economy? *(Chap 3, Class-XII, New NCERT)*

(a) Jan Dhan Yojana
(b) Aadhaar Enabled Payment Systems
(c) National Financial Switch
(d) All of the above

↗ *Ans. (d)*

Exp. All of the given schemes focusses on a cashless economy. Jan Dhan Yojana, Aadhar Enabled Payment Systems, National Financial Switch, E-wallets etc are some of the initiatives taken by the government to go cashless.

A cashless economy is such economy whereby financial transactions are not connected with money in the form of physical bank notes or coins but rather through the transfer of digital information between the transacting parties. In India, the government has taken these initiatives for greater financial inclusion.

5. Which of the following statements is incorrect?
(Chap 3, Class-XII, New NCERT)

(a) The larger is the quantum of transactions to be made, the larger is the quantity of money demanded.

(b) When interest rates go up, people become more interested in holding money.

(c) At higher interest rates, money demanded comes down.

(d) All are correct

↗ *Ans. (b)*

Exp. Statement (b) is incorrect because when interest rates go up, people become less (not more) interested in holding money. It is because holding money amounts to holding less of interest-earning deposits, and thus less interest received. Therefore, at higher interest rates, demand for money comes down.

6. If you withdraw ₹ 1,00,000 in cash from your Demand Deposit Account at your bank, what will be the immediate effect on aggregate money supply in the economy? *(Chap 3, Class-XII, New NCERT)*
(IAS Pre 2020)

(a) It will reduce it by ₹ 1,00,000.

(b) It will increase it by ₹ 1,00,000.

(c) It will increase it by more than ₹ 1,00,000.

(d) It will remain unchanged.

↗ *Ans. (d)*

Exp. The immediate effect would be a no change in the aggregate money supply in the economy.

The aggregate money supply in an economy can be expressed as $M = C + D$,

wherein 'C' is Currency with public

'D' is Demand Deposits by public with banks.

Now taking out ₹ 1 lakh from 'D' would increase same amount 'C' with public which will not impact the overall supply of money. The money supply is the total value of money available in the economy at a point of time.

7. To lower the interest rates, the RBI should
(Chap 3, Class-XII, New NCERT) (IAS Pre 2018)

(a) purchase securities

(b) decrease the money supply

(c) raise the treasury bill rate

(d) raise the reserve requirement

↗ *Ans. (a)*

Exp. To lower interest rates, the Reserve Bank of India (RBI) purchase securities. The open market purchase of securities by RBI increases the money supply in the economy, which lead to the decrease in interest rates as more money is available to the people.

The purchase and sale of securities by RBI in open market is one of the quantitative measures utilised by RBI to affect the money supply in the economy.

8. Which of the following institutions formulates the monetary policy in India?
(Chap 5, Class-IX & X, Old NCERT)

(a) NITI Aayog   (b) RBI

(c) Ministry of Finance   (d) SEBI

↗ *Ans. (b)*

Exp. Reserve Bank of India (RBI) formulates the monetary policy in India. This policy is periodically reviewed by RBI to achieve the goal of financial stability and the required level of liquidity in the economy. The RBI also controls and regulates the currency system of the economy of India.

9. Identify the incorrect statement regarding the Reserve Bank of India. *(Chap 3, Class-XII, New NCERT)*

(a) It was established in 1948.

(b) It issues the currency of the country. It controls the money supply of the country through various methods, like bank rate, open market operations and variations in reserve ratios.

(c) It acts as a banker to the government.

(d) It is the custodian of the foreign exchange reserves of the economy.

↗ *Ans. (a)*

Exp. Statement (a) is incorrect regarding the Reserve Bank of India as RBI was established in 1935. It is the Central bank of India. It is the sole issuer of currency notes in India. It controls the money supply of the country through various methods, such as

• It gives loans to commercial banks.

• Open market operations (buying and selling of bonds issued by the government in open market) to control inflation.

• It lends to Bank at all times and is said to be the lender of last resort.

It is also the custodian of the foreign exchange reserves of the economy and is vested with the responsibility of managing their investment.

10. **The banks are required to maintain a certain ratio between their cash in hand and total assets. This is called**

(Chap 3, Class-XII, New NCERT) (UPPSC Pre 2007)

(a) SLR
(b) CBR
(c) SBR
(d) CRR

➐ *Ans.* *(d)*

Exp. Cash Reserve Ratio (CRR) is the amount of funds that banks have to maintain with the RBI. It is calculated as ratio between their cash in hand and total assets. It is one of the Quantitative tool of monetary policy used by RBI to control money supply in the economy. The objective behind CRR is to ensure that the banks maintain a minimum level of liquidity against their liabilities.

11. **In India, the Repo Rate is announced by**

(Chap 3, Class-XII, New NCERT) (WBPSC Pre 2017)

(a) the Ministry of Finance, Government of India.
(b) the Prime Minister of India.
(c) the Reserve Bank of India.
(d) the President of India.

➐ *Ans.* *(c)*

Exp. In India, the Repo Rate is announced by the Reserve Bank of India (RBI). It is a type of repurchase agreement between RBI and commercial banks of the country for the sale/purchase of government securities. Repo Rate refers to the rate at which commercial banks borrow money by selling the securities to RBI to maintain liquidity in case of shortage of funds. In case of Reverse Repo, RBI borrows money from the banks when there is excess liquidity. The RBI conducts repo and reverse repo operation at various maturities : overnight, 7 days, 14 days etc.

12. **The difference between the interest rate paid by the banks to depositors and the rate charged from the borrowers is known as which of the following?** *(Chap 3, Class-X, New NCERT)*

(a) Margin
(b) Liquidity
(c) Spread
(d) Espionage

➐ *Ans.* *(c)*

Exp. The difference between the interest rate paid by the banks to depositors and the rate charged from the borrowers is known as 'spread'. Generally, the interest rate paid by the banks to depositors is lower than the rate charged from the borrowers. Spread is the profit appropriated by the bank.

13. **Consider the following statements about the tools used by RBI to control money supply.**

(Chap 3, Class-XII, New NCERT)

1. Banks are required to keep some reserves in liquid form in the short term known as Liquidity Adjustment Facility (LAF).
2. Cash Reserve Ratio (CRR) is the percentage of deposits which a bank must keep as cash reserves with the bank.

Which of the statement(s) given above is/are incorrect?

(a) Only 1
(b) Only 2
(c) Both 1 and 2
(d) Neither 1 nor 2

➐ *Ans.* *(a)*

Exp. Statement (1) is incorrect about the tools used by RBI to control money supply.

Banks are required to keep some reserves in liquid form in the short term. This ratio is called Statutory Liquidity Ratio (SLR) and not Liquidity Adjustment Facility (LAF). As of November, 2021, SLR is 18% on the other hand, Cash Reserve Ratio (CRR) is the percentage of deposits which a bank must keep as cash reserves with the bank. This is done to ensure that no bank is over lending. This is the legal requirement and is binding on the banks. As of November, 2021, CRR rate is 4%.

14. **Consider the following statements.**

(Chap 3, Class-XII, New NCERT)

1. Qualitative tools control the extent of money supply by changing the CRR, or bank rate or open market operations.
2. Quantitative tools include persuasion by the Central Bank in order to make commercial banks discourage or encourage lending which is done through moral suasion, margin requirement, etc.

Which of the statement(s) given above is/are incorrect?

(a) Only 1
(b) Only 2
(c) Both 1 and 2
(d) Neither 1 nor 2

➐ *Ans.* *(c)*

Exp. Both the statements (1) and (2) are incorrect.

The tools used by the Central Bank can be qualitative or quantitative. Quantitative tools control the extent of money supply by changing the Cash Reserve Ratio (CRR) or bank rate or open market operations. It is used either to increase or decrease the supply of money in the economy.

Qualitative tools for controlling the money supply by the Central Bank include persuasion by the Central Bank in order to make commercial banks discourage or encourage lending which is done through moral suasion, margin requirement etc.

15. **Which of the following statements is incorrect regarding Open Market Operations?**

(Chap 3, Class-XII, New NCERT)

(a) It refers to buying and selling of bonds issued by the Government in the open market.

(b) Selling of a bond to private individuals or institutions leads to reduction in the quantity of reserves.

(c) Outright open market operations are short term in nature.

(d) In Repo operation, when the Central bank buys the security, the agreement of purchase also has specification about date and price of resale of this security.

↗ *Ans.* *(c)*

Exp. Statement (c) is incorrect regarding Open Market Operations. There are two types of open market operations viz., outright and repo.

Open market operations refer to buying and selling of bonds issued by the government in open market. This purchase or sale is entrusted to the Central Bank on behalf of the government.

16. **The rate at which RBI gives loans to the commercial banks is known as which of the following?** *(Chap 3, Class-XII, New NCERT)*

(a) Marginal Stand Facility

(b) Marginal Rate

(c) Base Rate

(d) None of the above

↗ *Ans.* *(a)*

Exp. The rate at which RBI gives loans to the commercial banks is known as 'Marginal Stand Facility'. It is one of the tool to control the money supply by the Central Bank i.e RBI. By increasing the bank rate, loans taken by commercial banks become more expensive. This reduces the reserves held by the commercial bank and hence, decreases money supply. A fall in the bank rate can increase the money supply.

17. **Demonetisation of ₹ 500 and ₹ 1000 currency notes was announced on**

(Chap 3, Class-XII, New NCERT) (WBPSC Pre 2020)

(a) 8th November, 2016   (b) 1st January, 2017

(c) 15th August, 2016   (d) 31st March, 2017

↗ *Ans.* *(a)*

Exp. Demonetisation of ₹ 500 and ₹ 1000 currency notes was announced on 8th November, 2016. Under this reform, new currency notes of ₹ 500 and ₹ 2000 were launched. It was aimed to tackle the problem of corruption, black money, terrorism and circulation of fake money in the economy. It also increased tax compliances by shifting transactions out of the cash economy into the formal payment system.

18. **The money multiplier in an economy increases with which one of the following?**

(Chap 3, Class-XII, New NCERT) (IAS Pre 2021)

(a) Increase in the cash reserve ratio.

(b) Increase in the banking habit of the population.

(c) Increase in the statutory liquidity ratio.

(d) Increase in the population of the country.

↗ *Ans.* *(b)*

Exp. The money multipliers in an economy increases with increase in the banking habit of the population. Money multiplier is defined as the ratio of the stock of money to the stock of high powered money in an economy. With increased banking habits, the deposits in the banking system will increase, which then will increase the money multiplier.

19. **Consider the following statements.**

(Chap 3, Class-XII, New NCERT)

1. The Central bank may sell the securities through an agreement which has a specification about the date and price at which it will be repurchased called a reverse repurchase agreement or reverse repo.

2. The Reserve Bank of India conducts repo and reverse repo operations at various maturities i.e., overnight, 7 days, 14 days, etc.

Which of the statement(s) given above is/are correct?

(a) Only 1   (b) Only 2

(c) Both 1 and 2   (d) Neither 1 nor 2

↗ *Ans.* *(c)*

Exp. Both the statements (1) and (2) are correct.

The Central Bank may sell the securities through an agreement which has a specification about the date and price at which it will be repurchased. This type of agreement is called a reverse repurchase agreement or reverse repo. The rate at which the money is withdrawn in this manner is called as 'reverse repo rate'.

It is a type of open market operation and important tool to control the money supply. The present, reverse repo rate is 3.5%.

The Reserve Bank of India conducts repo and reverse repo operations at various maturities i.e., overnight, 7 days, 14 days etc. This type of operations have now become the main tool of monetary policy of the RBI.

20. Which of the following statements is incorrect regarding currency notes and coins?

(Chap 3, Class-XII, New NCERT)

(a) Currency notes and coins are called fiat money.

(b) They do not have intrinsic value like a gold or silver coin.

(c) They are also called legal tenders as they cannot be refused by any citizen of the country for settlement of any kind of transaction.

(d) Demand deposits like coins and notes are also legal tenders.

↗ *Ans.* *(d)*

Exp. Statement (d) is incorrect regarding currency notes and coins as demand deposits like coins and notes are not considered as legal tenders as they can be refused by anyone as a mode of payment.

Currency notes and coins do not have any intrinsic value like gold and silver but they derive the value from the guarantee provided by the issuing authority of these items. Therefore, they are also called as fiat money.

21. Which of the following statements is incorrect regarding measures of money?

(Chap 3, Class-XII, New NCERT)

(a) M_1 and M_2 are known as narrow money.

(b) M_3 and M_4 are known as broad money.

(c) M_1 is most liquid and easiest for transactions whereas M_4 is least liquid of all.

(d) M_2 is also known as aggregate monetary resources.

↗ *Ans.* *(d)*

Exp. Statement (d) is incorrect regarding measures of money.

M_2 is the currency with the Public + Demand Deposits with the Banking System + 'Other' Deposits with the RBI + Savings Deposits of Post-office Savings Banks. M_2 comes under narrow money, as it is most liquid after M_1.

M_3 is the most commonly used measure of money supply. It is also known as aggregate monetary resources.

It can be written as follows.

M_3 is equal to M_1 + Net time deposits of commercial banks.

M_1 and M_2 are known as Narrow money.

M_3 and M_4 are called as Broad money.

These measures are in decreasing order of liquidity. Therefore, M_1 is most liquid and easiest for transactions while M_4 is least liquid of all.

22. Which of the following statements regarding terms of credit is incorrect?

(Chap 3, Class-X, New NCERT)

(a) Interest rate, collateral and documentation requirement, and the mode of repayment together comprise, what is called the Terms of Credit.

(b) Collateral is an asset that the borrower owns and uses this as a guarantee to a lender until the loan is repaid.

(c) In case a borrower fails to repay the loan, the lender has the right to sell the asset or collateral to obtain payment only after the consent of the borrower.

(d) Property such as land titles, deposits with banks, livestock are some common examples of collateral used for borrowing.

↗ *Ans.* *(c)*

Exp. Statement (c) is incorrect regarding the terms of credit as in case a borrower fails to repay the loan, the lender has the right to sell the asset or collateral to obtain payment without the consent of the borrower. Collateral is an asset that the borrower owns and uses as a guarantee to lender until the loan is repaid. Property such as land, building, vehicle, livestock, deposits with banks etc are the examples of collateral.

Interest rates, collateral and documentation requirement and the mode of repayment together comprise the terms of credit. The terms of credit may vary depending on the nature of the lender and the borrower.

23. Which of the following monetary instruments has the highest liquidity? *(Chap 3, Class-XII, New NCERT)*

(a) Debenture

(b) Credit Note

(c) Currency

(d) Land or building

↗ *Ans.* *(c)*

Exp. Among the given monetary instruments, currency has the highest liquidity. It comes under the category of narrow money. Liquidity is the ability to convert an asset into cash and without losing money against the market price. In other words, it is an asset that can easily be converted into cash in a short duration of time. Currency, saving accounts, money market instruments, marketable securities etc. are some examples of liquid assets.

24. Consider the following statements regarding bank in India. *(Chap 3, Class XII, New NCERT)*

1. The NARCL is a part of a new Bad bank.

2. India now has 12 PSBs instead of 27 from April 2020.

3. EASE 4.0 is a common reform agenda for PSBs.

Which of the statement(s) given above is/are correct?

(a) 1 and 2   (b) 1, 2 and 3
(c) 2 and 3   (d) All of these

↗ *Ans.* *(d)*

Exp. All the statements (1), (2) and (3) are correct regarding bank in India. The National Asset Reconstruction Company Limited (NARCL) is a part of a new Bad bank structure that was announced in the Budget 2021. NARCL has been incorporated under the Companies Act. Public Sector Banks (PSBs) will maintain 51% ownership in NARCL.

The Government of India has merged 10 state-owned banks (PSBs) into four. India now has only 12 PSBs in April 2019 instead of 27 (in 2017).

Union Finance Minister undertook the annual performance review of the Public Sector Banks (PSBs) and launched the EASE 4.0 or Enhanced Access and Service Excellence Reform Agenda. EASE 4.0 is a common reform agenda for PSBs aimed at institutionalising clean and smart building.

25. **What is the term of short-term borrowing in the banking system?** *(Chap 7, Class-XII, Old NCERT)*

(a) 1 to 10 days   (b) 1 to 14 days
(c) 1 month   (d) 1 to 3 months

↗ *Ans.* *(b)*

Exp. The term of short-term borrowing in the banking system is from 1 to 14 days.

It can be classified into two categories – call and notice money. The money that is lent for one day in the market is called 'call money' and the short-term loan which exceeds one day but less than 14 days are referred as 'notice money'. Bank resorts to these types of loans to fill the asset liability mismatch, comply with the statutory Cash Reserve Ratio (CRR) and Statutory Liquidity Ratio (SLR) requirements and to meet sudden demand of funds.

26. **The Narasimham Committee is related to which of the following?** *(Chap 7, Class-XII, Old NCERT)*

(a) Fiscal Policy Reforms
(b) Banking Sector Reforms
(c) GST Reform
(d) Capital Account Convertibility

↗ *Ans.* *(b)*

Exp. The Narasimham Committee is related to Banking Sector Reforms. The committee focussed on various areas such as Capital adequacy, Bank mergers, Bank legislation etc. Some of its important recommendations are as follows

- It is considered as the stronger banking system in the context of the current account convertibility.
- It recommended the raising of capital adequacy ratio.
- It recommended the 'Narrow Banking Concept' where weak banks will be allowed to place their funds only in short term and risk free assets.

09

Fiscal Policy and Budget

Old NCERT Class IX & X (The State and Economic Development), **New NCERT Class XII** (Government Budget and Economy), **Old NCERT Class XII** (Economy and Government Budget)

1. Which of the following statements is incorrect regarding the Government Budget?

(Chap 5, Class-XII, New NCERT)

(a) The Annual Financial Statement constitutes the main budget document of the government.

(b) The statements that relate to the current financial year only are included in the revenue account.

(c) The statements that concern the assets and liabilities of the government are included into the capital account.

(d) None of the above

⬈ *Ans.* *(d)*

Exp. None of the given statement is incorrect regarding the Government Budget.

Article 112 of the Indian Constitution entrust responsibility to the government to present before the Parliament a statement of expenditures of the government in respect of every financial year. This Annual Financial Statement constitutes the main budget document of the government.

It is further divided into two accounts–revenue and capital account. The statements that relate to the current financial year only are included in revenue account and those financial statements that concern with the assets and liabilities of the government are included into capital account.

2. Which of the following is not one of the functions of the Government Budget in India?

(Chap 8, Class-XII, Old NCERT)

(a) Resource allocation

(b) Redistribution

(c) Stabilisation

(d) Inflation targeting

⬈ *Ans.* *(d)*

Exp. Inflation targeting is not one of the functions of the Government Budget in India. Inflation targeting means keeping the inflation rate within the manageable band. In India, inflation targeting is the primary function of Reserve Bank of India (RBI).

Resource allocation means responsibility of the government to provide certain goods and services which cannot be provided by the market mechanism. Through redistributive mechanisms (such as taxes, subsidies) government aims to bring financial inclusiveness in the society. The intervention of the government whether to expand demand or reduce, it constitutes the stabilisation function that is an essential component of budget in India.

3. Consider the following Assertion (A) and Reason (R) and choose the correct code.

(Chap 5, Class-XII, New NCERT)

Assertion (A) The government can change the distribution of income and bring about a distribution that is considered 'fair' by society.

Reason (R) The government sector affects the personal disposable income of households by making transfers and collecting taxes.

Codes

(a) Both A and R are true and R is the correct explanation of A.

(b) Both A and R are true, but R is not the correct explanation of A.

(c) A is true, but R is false.

(d) A is false, but R is true.

⬈ *Ans.* *(a)*

Exp. Both Assertion (A) and Reason (R) are true and Reason (R) is the correct explanation of Assertion (A).

Government through its redistribution mechanisms (such as taxes, subsidies, scholarships, etc) can change the distribution of income and bring about a distribution that is considered 'fair' by the society. It is one of the most important tool for achieving the goal of inclusive development.

Also through transfers (such as scholarship, grant, subsidies, etc.) and collecting taxes, the government affects the personal disposable income of households.

4. **Which of the following budgets introduced 'Gender Budgeting in India' for the first time?**

(Chap 5, Class-XII, New NCERT)

(a) Union Budget 2004-05
(b) Union Budget 2005-06
(c) Union Budget 2006-07
(d) Union Budget 2003-04

↗ *Ans.* *(b)*

Exp. The Union Budget 2005-06 introduced 'Gender Budgeting in India' for the first time. It is a budgeting tool which allows policymakers to allocate funds and direct expenditure keeping in mind the requirements of female in India. It ensures that the benefits of development reach women as much as men.

5. **Consider the following Assertion (A) and Reason (R) and choose the correct code.**

(Chap 5, Class-IX & X, Old NCERT)

Assertion (A) Revenue receipts are termed as non-redeemable.

Reason (R) Revenue receipts are those receipts that do not lead to a claim on the government.

Codes

(a) Both A and R are true and R is the correct explanation of A.
(b) Both A and R are true, but R is not the correct explanation of A.
(c) A is true, but R is false.
(d) A is false, but R is true.

↗ *Ans.* *(a)*

Exp. Both Assertion (A) and Reason (R) are true and Reason (R) is the correct explanation of Assertion (A). Revenue receipts are termed as non-redeemable. They are always recurring in nature and do not have a direct impact on the assets and liabilities of the government.

Also these receipts do not lead to a claim on the government. Tax revenues are an important component of revenue receipts.

6. **Consider the following statements about revenue receipts.** *(Chap 5, Class-XII, New NCERT)*

1. They are divided into tax and non-tax revenues.
2. Tax revenues have been divided into direct taxes and indirect taxes like excise taxes, customs duties and GST.

Which of the statement(s) given above is/are correct?

(a) Only 1
(b) Only 2
(c) Both 1 and 2
(d) Neither 1 nor 2

↗ *Ans.* *(c)*

Exp. Both the statements (1) and (2) are correct regarding revenue receipts.

Those receipts that do not lead to claim on the government and are recurring in nature are termed as revenue receipts. They are divided into tax and non-tax revenues.

Tax revenue have been further divided into direct tax like income tax, corporation tax and indirect taxes like excise taxes, custom duties and service tax. Non-tax revenue constitutes dividends and profits on investment made by government, fees and other receipts rendered by the government.

7. **Consider the following statements regarding non-debt creating capital receipts.**

(Chap 5, Class-XII, New NCERT)

1. Non-debt creating capital receipts are those receipts which are not borrowings and, therefore, do not give rise to debt.
2. Recovery of loans and the proceeds from the sale of PSUs are examples of non-debt creating capital receipts.

Which of the statement(s) given above is/are incorrect?

(a) Only 1
(b) Only 2
(c) Both 1 and 2
(d) Neither 1 nor 2

↗ *Ans.* *(d)*

Exp. Neither statement (1) nor (2) is incorrect regarding non-debt creating capital receipts.

All those receipts of the government which create liability or reduce financial assets are termed as capital receipts. They may or may not create debts.

Non-debt creating capital receipts are those receipts which are not borrowings and therefore, do not give rise to debt. The recovery of loans and the proceeds from the sale of Public Sector Undertaking (PSUs) are some of the examples of non-debt creating capital receipts. It is useful in calculating the fiscal deficit.

8. Which of the following is not an example of Non-Tax Revenue? *(Chap 5, Class-XII, New NCERT)*

(a) Interest receipts

(b) Estate duty

(c) Fees

(d) Dividends and Profits on Investments

➤ *Ans. (b)*

Exp. Estate duty is not an example of Non-Tax Revenue. Estate duty is a type of direct tax and comes under tax revenue of the government. In India, it was introduced in the year 1953 as inheritance tax. It was abolished by the government in 1985.

Non-tax revenue of the government mainly consists of interest receipts on account of loans by the government, dividends and profits on investments made by the government, fees and other receipts for services rendered by the government. Cash, Grants-in-Aid from foreign countries and international organisations are also included in non-tax revenue receipts.

9. Which of the following do not form the part of Paper Tax? *(Chap 8, Class-XII, Old NCERT)*

(a) Entertainment Tax

(b) Wealth Tax

(c) Gift Tax

(d) Estate Duty

➤ *Ans. (a)*

Exp. Entertainment Tax do not form the part of Paper Tax. It is a type of indirect tax and constitutes important segment of revenue receipts of the government. It is subsumed under the Goods and Services Tax (GST).

The direct taxes like Wealth Tax, Gift Tax and Estate Duty (now abolished) have never, brought in large amount of revenue and thus have been referred to as Paper Taxes.

10. Interest payment is an item of

(Chap 5, Class-XII, New NCERT) (BPSC Pre 2015)

(a) revenue expenditure

(b) capital expenditure

(c) borrowing

(d) None of the above

➤ *Ans. (a)*

Exp. Interest payment is an item of revenue expenditure. Those expenditures incurred for purposes other than the creation of physical or financial assets are called Revenue expenditure.

It is generally used for normal functioning of the government department and provisions of basic services. Besides interest payments, defence services, subsidies, salaries and pensions are also included as the part of Revenue expenditure.

11. One of the most significant Fiscal policy objectives in India is to bring the revenue expenditures and receipts to the same level. Which of the following steps will help to achieve that objective? *(Chap 5, Class-XII, New NCERT)*

(a) The efforts to raise the total profits for public sector units.

(b) The efforts to improve the revenues from tax collection.

(c) The efforts to slow the growth rate for expenditures in the country.

(d) All of the above

➤ *Ans. (d)*

Exp. All the given steps will help to achieve that objective. Fiscal policy is an estimate of taxation and government expending that impacts the economy. The key objectives of fiscal policy are economic stability, price stability, full employment, optimum allocation of resources, accelerating the rate of economical development, capital formation and growth.

12. Which of the following items is classified as a Capital Receipt in the budget for the Government of India? *(Chap 5, Class-XII, New NCERT)*

(a) The borrowing made by the government from the public.

(b) The receipts from the collection of income tax.

(c) The dividends and profits received from the public sector units.

(d) The interest receipts for loans given by the government to its debt.

➤ *Ans. (a)*

Exp. Among the given statements, the borrowing made by the government from the public is classified as a Capital Receipt in the budget for the Government of India.

Capital receipts are loans taken by the government from the public, borrowings from foreign countries and institutions and borrowings from the Reserve Bank of India (RBI).

Recovery of loans given by the centre to states and others is also included in capital receipts. The capital receipt has a nature of non-recurrence.

13. Which of the following is the definition of a budget deficit? *(Chap 5, Class-XII, New NCERT)*

(a) Excess of the total expenditure over the total receipts minus interest payments and borrowings.

(b) Excess of the total expenditure over the total receipts minus borrowings.

(c) Excess of the revenue receipts.

(d) Excess of the total expenditure over the total receipts.

➚ *Ans.* (*d*)

Exp. Statement (d) is the correct definition of a budget deficit.

A budget deficit occurs when expenditures surpass revenue and then impacts the financial health of a country.

The term 'Budget deficit' is generally used when talking about total economic spending rather than the budget of businesses or individuals.

National debt is made of the accrued deficits in budget.

14. **Expenditure of the government which result in the creation of physical or financial assets or reduction in financial liabilities is known as which of the following?** *(Chap 5, Class-XII, New NCERT)*

(a) Plan Expenditure   (b) Non-Plan Expenditure
(c) Capital Expenditure   (d) Revenue Expenditure

➚ *Ans.* (*c*)

Exp. Expenditure of the government which result in creation of physical or financial assets or reduction in financial liabilities is known as Capital Expenditure. It includes expenditure on the acquisition of land, building, machinery, investment in shares, and loans and advances by the Central Government to State and Union Territory governments, Public Sector Undertakings (PSUs) and other parties.

15. **Which of the following expenditures is not an example of Capital expenditure?**
(Chap 8, Class-XII, Old NCERT)

(a) Acquisition of Land   (b) Investment in Shares
(c) Loans and Advances   (d) Grant-in-Aid

➚ *Ans.* (*d*)

Exp. Grant-in-Aid is not an example of Capital expenditure. It is classified under Revenue expenditure of the government which are incurred for purposes other than creation of physical and financial assets.

Those expenditures of the government which result in creation of physical or financial assets or reduction in financial liabilities are termed as capital expenditure. Acquisition of land, investment in shares, loans and advances are some of the examples of capital expenditure.

16. **Which of the following statements is incorrect?**
(Chap 5, Class-XII, New NCERT)

(a) Capital expenditure includes interest payments on debt incurred by the government and grants given to state governments and other parties.
(b) Budget documents classify total expenditure into plan and non-plan expenditure.
(c) Plan revenue expenditure relates to central plans and central assistance for State and Union Territory plans.
(d) Non-plan expenditure covers a vast range of general, economic and social services of the government.

➚ *Ans.* (*a*)

Exp. Statement (a) is incorrect as interest payments on debt incurred by the government and grants given to state governments and other parties are included in revenue expenditure not in capital expenditure.

It is usually incurred for purposes other than the creation of physical or financial assets of the government. Expenditure on acquisition of land, building, machinery, investment in shares and loans and advances by the Central government to state and UTs, PSUs and other parties come under capital expenditure.

17. **Consider the following statements about Budgetary Deficits.** *(Chap 5, Class-XII, New NCERT)*

1. The revenue deficit refers to the excess of government's revenue expenditure over revenue receipts.
2. Primary deficit is the difference between the government's total expenditure and its total receipts excluding borrowing.

Which of the statement(s) given above is/are incorrect?

(a) Only 1   (b) Only 2
(c) Both 1 and 2   (d) Neither 1 nor 2

➚ *Ans.* (*b*)

Exp. Statement (2) is incorrect regarding Budgetary Deficits. It is a financial condition wherein the expenditure of the government exceeds its revenue. Primary deficit is the fiscal deficit minus (deduction) the interest payment and helps in focussing the present fiscal imbalances of the government.

18. **Fiscal Deficit is** *(Chap 5, Class-XII, New NCERT)*
(WBPSC Pre 2018)

(a) Revenue Receipts + Capital Receipts (only recoveries of loans and other receipts) – Total Expenditure.
(b) Budget Deficits + Government's market borrowings and liabilities.
(c) Primary Deficit + Interest payments.
(d) All of the above

➚ *Ans.* (*a*)

Exp. Fiscal Deficit is Revenue Receipts + Capital Receipts (only recoveries of loans and other receipts) – Total Expenditure.

Fiscal Deficit is the difference between the government's total expenditure and its total receipts excluding borrowing. It indicates the total borrowing requirements of the government from all sources.

19. Which of the following statements is incorrect regarding the features of the Fiscal Responsibility and Budget Management (FRBM) Act? *(Chap 5, Class-XII, New NCERT)*

(a) The Act mandates the Central government to take appropriate measures to reduce revenue deficit to not more than 3% of GDP and to eliminate the Fiscal Deficit.

(b) The actual deficits may exceed the targets specified only on grounds of national security or natural calamity.

(c) The Reserve Bank of India must not subscribe to the primary issues of Central government securities from the year 2006-07.

(d) Quarterly review of the trends in receipts and expenditure in relation to the budget be placed before both the Houses of Parliament.

↗ *Ans.* (a)

Exp. Statement (a) is incorrect regarding Fiscal Responsibility and Budget Management (FRBM) Act. The act promulgated in 2003, institutionally binds the Central government to take appropriate measures to reduce Fiscal Deficit (not Revenue Deficit) to not more than 3% of GDP and to eliminate revenue deficit by 31st March, 2009 and thereafter build up adequate revenue surplus. It also mandated reduction in Fiscal Deficit by 0.3% of GDP each year and the revenue deficit by 0.5%. This Act was amended in 2018.

20. Alongwith the budget, which of the following policy statements are mandated by the Fiscal Responsibility and Budget Management (FRBM) Act, 2003? *(Chap 5, Class-XII, New NCERT)*

1. Medium-term Fiscal Policy Statement
2. The Fiscal Policy Strategy Statement
3. The Macroeconomic Framework Statement
4. Short-term Fiscal Policy Statement

Codes

(a) 1 and 4   (b) 1, 2 and 3

(c) 1 and 2   (d) 1, 2, 3 and 4

↗ *Ans.* (b)

Exp. Statements (1), (2) and (3) are mandated by the Fiscal Responsibility and Budget Management (FRBM) Act, 2003. It mandated the government to place in Parliament a medium term fiscal policy statement, the fiscal policy strategy statement and macroeconomic framework statement along with the budget in Parliament.

It helps in following a prudent fiscal policy and ensuring inter-generational equity and long-term macroeconomic stability by achieving sufficient revenue surplus.

21. Alongwith the Budget, the Finance Minister also places other documents before the Parliament which includes 'The Macroeconomic Framework Statement'. The aforesaid document is presented because this is mandated by

(Chap 5, Class-XII, New NCERT) (IAS Pre 2020)

(a) Long standing Parliament convention.

(b) Article 112 and Article 110(1) of the Constitution of India.

(c) Article 113 of the Constitution of India.

(d) Provisions of the Fiscal Responsibility and Budget Management Act, 2003.

↗ *Ans.* (d)

Exp. Financial Responsibility and Budget Management Act, 2003 mandated to place 'The Macroeconomic Framework Statement' along with Budget before the Parliament.

This Act aims towards ensuring long-term macroeconomic stability and inter-generational equity by creating statutory basis for effective debt management. It also contains legislative provisions directing the government to reduce Fiscal and Revenue Deficit and to follow a policy of fiscal prudence.

22. Consider the following statements with respect to the Goods and Services Tax (GST).

(Chap 5, Class-XII, New NCERT)

1. Goods and Services Tax (GST) is the single comprehensive indirect tax, operational from 1st July, 2017, on supply of goods and services from the manufacturer to the consumer.

2. It is a source based consumption tax with the facility of Input Tax Credit in the supply chain.

Which of the statement(s) given above is/are incorrect?

(a) Only 1

(b) Only 2

(c) Both 1 and 2

(d) Neither 1 nor 2

↗ *Ans.* (b)

Exp. Statement (2) is incorrect regarding GST as it is a destination based (not source based) consumption tax with the facility of Input Tax Credit in the supply chain.

Goods and Services Tax (GST) is a Value Added Tax levied on most goods and services sold for domestic consumption. GST is paid by consumers, but it is remitted to the government by the businesses selling the goods and services.

23. The 'Goods and Services Tax' was proposed by a task force, whose President was

(Chap 5, Class-XII, New NCERT) (MPPSC Pre 2017)

(a) Vijay Kelkar (b) Montek Singh Ahluwalia
(c) Arun Jaitley (d) Narasimha

↗ *Ans.* (a)

Exp. The 'Goods and Services Tax' was proposed by a task force, whose President was Vijay Kelkar. This task force in 2004, suggested a single comprehensive tax, GST, to simplify indirect tax mechanism and to remove cascading effect of taxation in India.

GST is operational in India from 1st July, 2017 and is destination based consumption tax with facility of Input Tax Credit in the supply chain.

24. Which among the following taxes has not been subsumed under the GST?

(Chap 5, Class-XII, New NCERT) (CGPSC Pre 2020)

(a) Custom Tax (b) Value Added Tax
(c) Service Tax (d) Entry Tax

↗ *Ans.* (a)

Exp. Among the given taxes, custom tax has not been subsumed under the GST. Custom tax is a type of indirect tax levied on goods which are imported into India.

Apart from Custom Tax, Minimum Alternate Tax (MAT) has also not been subsumed under the GST. MAT is a type of direct tax introduced in 1996 which includes all companies in the income tax loop. It helps in limiting tax exemptions availed by companies.

25. Which of the following statements is not one of the advantages of the GST?

(Chap 5, Class-XII, New NCERT)

(a) GST has simplified the multiplicity of taxes on goods and services.
(b) It has facilitated the freedom of movement of goods and services and created a common market in the country.

(c) It is aimed at increasing the cascading effect of various taxes on consumers.
(d) It has also reduced the overall cost of production, which will make Indian products/services more competitive in the domestic and international markets.

↗ *Ans.* (c)

Exp. Statement (c) is not one of the advantages of GST as it is aimed at eliminating the cascading (not increasing) effect of various taxes on consumers.

GST, which subsumed almost all domestic indirect taxes under one head, is perhaps the biggest tax reform in the history of independent India. It was launched in operation on the midnight of 1st July, 2017.

It has achieved it by amalgamating large number of central and state taxes and cesses which were levied on various stages of production.

26. Consider the following statements with respect to the Goods and Services Tax.

(Chap 5, Class-XII, New NCERT)

1. State Governments will continue to levy VAT on alcoholic liquor for human consumption.
2. Under GST, there are 5 standard rates applied i.e. 0%, 5%, 12%,18% and 28% on supply of all goods or services across the country.

Which of the statement(s) given above is/are correct?

(a) Only 1 (b) Only 2
(c) Both 1 and 2 (d) Neither 1 nor 2

↗ *Ans.* (c)

Exp. Both the statements (1) and (2) are correct with respect to the GST, as it allows state governments to levy VAT (Value Added Tax) on alcoholic liquor for human consumption. Petroleum products also has been kept out from the ambit of GST.

As of December 2021, there are 5 GST rates slab operational in the country, i.e 0%, 5%, 12%, 18% and 28% on supply of all goods and services across the country.

10

International Trade and Balance of Payment

Old NCERT Class IX & X (Towards Economic Development), New NCERT Class-X (Globalisation and the Indian Economy), New NCERT Class XI (Indian Economy on the Eve of Independence), New NCERT Class XI (Indian Economy 1950-1990), New NCERT Class XII (Open Economy : Macroeconomics), Old NCERT Class XII (Balance of Payment), Old NCERT Class XII (Foreign Exchange Rates : Meaning and Assessment)

1. **Which ministry of Government of India is responsible for India's Foreign Trade Policy?**
(Chap 10, Class XII, Old NCERT) (MPPSC Pre 2020)
(a) Defence (b) External Affairs
(c) Commerce and Industry (d) Home Affairs

➤ **Ans.** *(c)*

Exp. The Union Ministry of Commerce and Industry is responsible for India's Foreign Trade Policy. This policy is usually implemented for five years and provides road map for boosting exports from India.

The latest Foreign Trade Policy (for 2021-2026) had assigned significant role to districts in promoting foreign trade from India.

2. **Which of the following statements is incorrect regarding an open trade?** *(Chap 4, Class-X, New NCERT)*
(a) Choice of goods in the markets rises.
(b) Prices of the same goods in the two markets tend to become equal.
(c) The cost differential of producing a commodity discourages trade between countries.
(d) All are correct

➤ **Ans.** *(c)*

Exp. Statement (c) is incorrect regarding an open trade because the reason behind increase in trade between countries is the cost differential of producing a commodity. It refers to export of good which is cost effective to produce and import of good which is expensive to produce in the country but cheap in other countries. Factors of production such as land, labour, resources etc affect the cost of production and those countries characterised by abundance of these resources are able to increase their share in foreign export.

3. **Which of the following Statement(s) is/are correct regarding foreign trade?**
(Chap 4, Class-IX & X, Old NCERT)
(a) The Balance of Trade (BoT) is the difference between the monetary value of a nation's exports and imports of goods and services in a particular year.
(b) If exports are more than imports, then the balance of trade is positive.
(c) In case of imports higher than exports, there is decline in foreign exchange reserves.
(d) All of the above

➤ **Ans.** *(d)*

Exp. All the given statements (a), (b) and (c) are correct regarding the foreign trade.

Balance of Trade (BoT) is the difference between the value of exports and the value of imports of goods of a country in a given period of time. It is also known as Trade Balance.

With reference to balance sheet, it can be positive, negative or balanced. When exports and imports are equal, it is considered balanced. When exports are greater than imports, the Balance of trade is positive. Similarly, it is negative when imports surpass the exports. In case, imports are higher than exports, there is decline in foreign exchange reserve whereas higher exports than imports leads to increase in foreign exchange reserves.

4. **Identify the incorrect statement regarding the features of Special Economic Zone (SEZ).**

(Chap 4, Class-X, New NCERT)

(a) To attract foreign companies to invest in India, Industrial zones called Special Economic Zones (SEZs), are being set up.

(b) Companies who set up production units in the SEZs do not have to pay taxes for an initial period of five years.

(c) Instead of hiring workers on a part time basis, companies hire workers 'flexibly' for longer periods.

(d) Government has also allowed flexibility in the labour laws to attract foreign investment.

⌐ *Ans. (c)*

Exp. Statement (c) is incorrect regarding Special Economic Zone (SEZ) as in this zone companies hire workers for short periods when there is intense pressure of work.

Special Economic Zone (SEZ) are one of the innovative steps by Government to attract foreign companies to invest in India.

Special Economic Zone is an area which is set up to incentivise businesses. SEZs offer competitive infrastructure, duty free exports, tax incentives and other measures designed to make production cheaper and exports more competitive.

5. **Consider the following statements regarding Foreign Trade of India in the British era.**

(Chap 1, Class-XI, New NCERT)

1. More than half of India's foreign trade was restricted to Britain while the rest was allowed with a few other countries like China, Ceylon (Sri Lanka) and Persia (Iran).

2. India's economy under the British colonial rule remained fundamentally service oriented.

Which of the statement(s) given above is/are correct?

(a) Only 1   (b) Only 2

(c) Both 1 and 2   (d) Neither 1 nor 2

⌐ *Ans. (a)*

Exp. Statement (1) is correct regarding Foreign Trade of India in the British era.

Restrictive policies of commodity production, trade and tariff pursued by the colonial government adversely affected the structure, composition and volume of India's Foreign Trade. As a result, India became exporter of primary goods and importer of finished goods; further more than half of India's foreign trade was restricted to Britain while the rest was allowed with a few other countries like China, Ceylon (Sri Lanka) and Persia (Iran).

Statement (2) is incorrect as India's economy under the British colonial rule remained fundamentally agrarian (not service oriented). About 85% of the country's population lived mostly in villages and derived livelihood directly or indirectly from agriculture.

6. **Which one of the following measures is not likely to aid in improving India's Balance of Payment position?** *(Chap 10, Class-XII, New NCERT) (BPSC Pre 2018)*

(a) Promotion of Import Substitution Policy.

(b) Devaluation of Rupee.

(c) Imposition of Higher Tariff on Imports.

(d) Levying of Higher Duties on Exports.

⌐ *Ans. (d)*

Exp. Levying of higher duties on exports is not likely to aid in improving India's Balance of Payment position. It will make exports costlier, thereby decreasing competitiveness of India's trade with the rest of the world.

Promotion of Import Substitution Policy will help in decreasing imports, devaluation of rupee will support exports from India and imposition of higher tariff on imports will discourage imports of goods and services in economy.

7. **Consider the following statements.**

(Chap 2, Class-XI, New NCERT)

1. Import Substitution aimed at replacing or substituting exports with domestic production.

2. Protection from imports took two forms - tariffs and quotas.

Which of the statement(s) given above is/are incorrect?

(a) Only 1   (b) Only 2

(c) Both 1 and 2   (d) Neither 1 nor 2

⌐ *Ans. (a)*

Exp. Statement (1) is incorrect as import substitution followed by India after independence aimed at replacing or substituting imports with domestic production. It helps in protecting the domestic firms from foreign competition.

8. **With reference to 'Balance of Payment', which of the following statement(s) is/are correct?**

(Chap 6, Class-XII, New NCERT)

1. It records transactions in goods and services only.

2. Transfer payments are receipts which the resident of a country receives for free.

Codes

(a) Only 1   (b) Only 2

(c) Both 1 and 2   (d) Neither 1 nor 2

⌐ *Ans. (b)*

Exp. Statement (2) is correct regarding the 'Balance of Payment' as transfer payments are receipts, which the resident of a country receives 'for free', without having to make any present or future payment in return. They consist of remittances, gifts and grants.

Statement (1) is incorrect regarding Balance of Payment as it records the transaction of goods, services and assets between residents of a country with the rest of the world for a specified time period typically a year.

9. The Balance of Payment of an economy is a systematic record of which of the following?
(Chap 10, Class-XII, Old NCERT) (IAS Pre 2013)
(a) All economic transactions between residents of a country and the rest of the world in a given period.
(b) Movement of capital from one country to another.
(c) Economic transaction between the governments of two countries.
(d) Capital movements from one country to another.

↗ *Ans.* (a)

Exp. The Balance of Payment of an economy is a systematic record of all economic transactions (goods, services and assets) between residents of a country and the rest of the world in a given period.

There are two main accounts in the Balance of Payment (BoP) – the current account and the capital account.

The current account records exports and imports in goods and services and transfer payments. The capital account records all international purchases and sales of assets such as money, stocks, bonds, etc.

10. Which of the following forms part of the Current Account of the Balance of Payment?
(Chap 10, Class-XII, Old NCERT)
1. Trade Balance
2. Foreign Asset
3. Invisibles
4. Special Drawing Rights

Codes
(a) 1, 2 and 4   (b) 1 and 3
(c) 2 and 4   (d) 1, 2, 3 and 4

↗ *Ans.* (b)

Exp. Trade balance and invisibles form the part of the Current Account of Balance of Payment. In this account, trade in services denoted as invisible trade because they are not seen to cross national borders.

The current account of the balance of payments includes a country's key activity, such as capital markets and services. The four major components of a current account are goods, services, income and current transfers.

11. Balance of payments is an accounting statement that records the economic transactions between
(Chap 6, Class-XII, New NCERT)
(a) residents of a country and non-resident individuals.
(b) residents of a country and rest of the world.
(c) Non-residents and rest of the world.
(d) None of the above

↗ *Ans.* (b)

Exp.

The Balance of Payments is an accounting statement that records the economic transaction between residents of a country and rest of the world because it is the difference between all money flowing into the country in a particular period of time and the outflow of money to the rest of the world.

The Balance of Payments consists of three main components i.e., current account, capital account and financial account.

12. Balance of Trade is   *(Chap 4, Class-IX & X, Old NCERT)*
(a) difference between export and import of goods.
(b) sum total of export and import of goods.
(c) difference between export and import of services.
(d) sum total of export and import services.

↗ *Ans.* (a)

Exp. The Balance of Trade is the difference between the value of a country's exports and the value of its imports. Formula for Balance of Trade is

Balance of Trade = Country's Exports

                   – Country's Imports

The Balance of Trade can be of three types
(i) Favourable balance (Surplus),
(ii) Unfavourable balance (Deficit) and
(iii) Equilibrium balance

13. Which of the following constitute Capital Account? *(Chap 10, Class-XII, Old NCERT) (IAS Pre 2013)*
1. Foreign Loans
2. Foreign Direct Investment
3. Private Remittances
4. Portfolio Investment

Codes
(a) 1, 2 and 3   (b) 1, 2 and 4
(c) 2, 3 and 4   (d) 1, 3 and 4

↗ *Ans.* (b)

Exp. Foreign Loans, Foreign Direct Investment and Portfolio Investment constitute Capital Account.

It records all international purchases and sales of assets such as currency, stocks, bonds etc. The Capital account balance of a country is equal to capital flows from the rest of the world, minus capital flows to the rest of the world. Private remittances are constituent of current account which is sum of the balance of merchandise trade, services and net transfers received from rest of the world.

14. **Consider the following statements.**

(Chap 10, Class XII, New NCERT)

1. According to new classification of BoP accounts, the transactions are divided into three accounts.
2. Current Account deficit is measured as a percentage of GDP.
3. Capital Account records all international transactions of assets.

Which of the statement(s) given above is/are correct?

Codes

(a) 1, 2 and 3   (b) 2 and 3   (c) 1 and 3   (d) 1 and 2

↗ *Ans.* (a)

Exp. All the given statements (1), (2) and (3) are correct. RBI made changes in the structure of Balance of Payments (BoP) accounts. According to the new classification, the transactions are divided into three accounts i.e., Current account, Financial Account and Capital account. All the transactions arising on account of trade in financial assets such as bonds and equity shares are now placed in the financial accounts.

There is a deficit in current account if the value of the goods and services imported exceeds, the value of those exported. Current Account Deficit is measured as a percentage of GDP. Capital Account records all international transactions of assets. Purchase of assets is a debit item on capital account. The Sale of assets is a credit items on the capital account.

15. **The indices of Normal Effective Exchange Rate and Real Effective Exchange Rate are used as indicators of**   *(Chap 10, Class XII, Old NCERT)*

(a) clean floating
(b) external competitiveness
(c) account convertibility
(d) capital inflow

↗ *Ans.* (b)

Exp. The indices of Normal Effective Exchange Rate (NEER) and Real Effective Exchange Rate (REER) are used as indicators of external competitiveness.

NEER is the weighted average of bilateral nominal exchange rates of the home currency in terms of foreign currencies.

The REER, defined as a weighted average of nominal exchange rates adjusted for relative price differential

between the domestic and foreign countries, relates to the Purchasing Power Parity (PPP) Hypothesis. It measures the international competitiveness of a country in international trade.

16. **Which of the following is/are included in the Foreign Exchange Reserves?**

(Chap 10, Class-XII, Old NCERT)

1. Foreign Currency
2. Gold
3. Special Drawing Rights
4. Foreign Securities

Codes

(a) 1, 2, 3 and 4   (b) 1 and 3
(c) 2 and 4   (d) 1, 3 and 4

↗ *Ans.* (a)

Exp. Foreign Currency, Gold, Special Drawing Rights (SDR) and Foreign Securities are included in the Foreign Exchange Reserves of the country.

These assets are held by nation's Central Bank or monetary authority (RBI in case of India).

Special drawing rights are supplementary foreign currency assets maintained by IMF, a country can borrow it from IMF during a balance of payment crisis. It is helpful in meeting any adverse scenario in case of Balance of Payment crisis and limiting external vulnerability.

17. **Consider the following statements about the Foreign Exchange Rate.**   *(Chap 6, Class-XII, New NCERT)*

1. Foreign Exchange Rate is the price of one currency in terms of another.
2. It links the currencies of different countries and enables comparison of international costs and prices.

Which of the statement(s) given above is/are correct?

(a) Only 1   (b) Only 2
(c) Both 1 and 2   (d) Neither 1 nor 2

↗ *Ans.* (c)

Exp. Both the statements (1) and (2) are correct regarding Foreign Exchange Rate. The price of one currency in terms of the other is known as the exchange rate. It can also be defined as the amount of domestic currency required to buy one unit of foreign currency. In foreign exchange market, national currencies are traded for one another.

The major participants in this market are commercial banks, foreign exchange brokers and other authorised dealers and the monetary authorities. Foreign exchange market links the currencies of different countries and enables comparison of international costs and prices.

18. **Which of the following statement is not correct about the Foreign Exchange Rate?**

(Chap 6, Class-XII, New NCERT)

(a) It can be determined through Flexible Exchange Rate, Fixed Exchange Rate or Managed Floating Exchange Rate.

(b) Flexible Exchange Rate is determined by the market forces of demand and supply.

(c) In the Dirty Floating Exchange Rate System, the government fixes the exchange rate at a particular level.

(d) Under the Managed Floating System, Central Banks intervene to buy and sell foreign currencies in an attempt to moderate exchange rate movements whenever they feel that such actions are appropriate.

↗ *Ans.* *(c)*

Exp. Statement (c) is not correct about the Foreign Exchange Rate. The Managed Floating System of Exchange Rate is also called Dirty Floating Exchange Rate system. Under this system, Central Banks intervene to buy and sell foreign currencies in an attempt to moderate exchange rate movements whenever they feel that such actions are appropriate. It is a mixture of a Flexible Exchange Rate System (the float part) and a Fixed Rate System (the managed part).

19. **Convertibility of rupee implies**

(Chap 6, Class-XII, New NCERT) (IAS Pre 2015)

(a) being able to convert rupee notes into gold.

(b) allowing the value of rupee to be fixed by market forces.

(c) freely permitting the conversion of rupee to other currencies and vice-versa.

(d) developing an international market for currencies in India.

↗ *Ans.* *(c)*

Exp. Convertibility of rupee implies freely permitting the conversion of rupee to other currencies and vice-versa. India adopted full current account convertibility since 1993, permitting individuals and entities to convert Indian rupee into foreign currency.

This was after India accepted the status and obligations of International Monetary Fund (IMF). India has allowed only partial capital account convertibility of rupee. It implies partial freedom of currency conversion related to capital inflows and outflows.

20. **Consider the following statements regarding Fixed Exchange Rate system.** *(Chap 6, Class-XII, New NCERT)*

1. In a Fixed Exchange Rate System, when some government action increases, the exchange rate is called Revaluation.

2. Devaluation is said to occur when the government decreases the exchange rate in a Fixed Exchange Rate System.

Which of the statement(s) given above is/are incorrect?

(a) Only 1

(b) Only 2

(c) Both 1 and 2

(d) Neither 1 nor 2

↗ *Ans.* *(c)*

Exp. Both the statements (1) and (2) are incorrect regarding Fixed Exchange Rate System.

Fixed Exchange Rate System is also known as Pegged Exchange Rate System and is characterised by devaluation and revaluation of the currency. A devaluation is said to occur when the exchange rate is increased by government action under a Pegged Exchange Rate System. Devaluation makes domestic currency cheaper.

Where as revaluation is said to occur, when the government decreases the exchange rate, thereby making domestic currency costlier.

The opposite of devaluation is revaluation wherein upward adjustment to a country's official exchange rate relative to a chosen baseline, such as wage rates, the price of gold, or a foreign currency is observed.

21. **Which of the following is not one of the advantages of the Flexible Exchange Rate system?** *(Chap 6, Class-XII, New NCERT)*

(a) The Flexible Exchange Rate System resolves problem of under valuation and overvaluation of currency.

(b) Government needs to maintain large stocks of foreign exchange reserves.

(c) Movements in the exchange rate automatically take care of the surpluses and deficits in the BoP.

(d) Countries gain independence in conducting their monetary policies, since they do not have to intervene to maintain exchange rates which are automatically taken care of by the market.

↗ *Ans.* *(b)*

Exp. Statement (b) is not one of the advantages of the Flexible Exchange Rate System.

In the Flexible Exchange Rate System, it is not necessary for the government to maintain a large stock of foreign exchange reserve.

The major advantage of flexible exchange rate is that movements in the exchange rate automatically take care of the surpluses and deficits in the BoP.

This exchange rate is determined by the market forces of demand and supply and is also known as Floating Exchange Rate.

This implies that countries gain independence in conducting their monetary policies, since they do not have to intervene to maintain exchange rates which are automatically taken care of by the market.

22. **Which of the following is also known as Paper Gold?** *(Chap 6, Class-XII, New NCERT) (UPPSC Pre 2004)*

(a) Government Security

(b) Treasury Bills

(c) P-Notes

(d) Special Drawing Rights

↗ *Ans.* *(d)*

Exp. Special Drawing Rights is also known as Paper Gold. The SDR is an international reserve asset, created by the IMF in 1969 to supplement its member countries' official reserves.

The value of the SDR is calculated from a weighted basket of major currencies, including the US Dollar, the Euro, Japanese Yen, Chinese Yuan and British Pound.

It was represented as an asset that could be used to offset Balance of Payment deficits in the same manner as gold or reserve currencies and hence, it is called as Paper Gold.

23. **Which of the following statements is incorrect regarding the External Sector?**

(Chap 6, Class-XII, New NCERT)

(a) The open economy multiplier is smaller than that in a closed economy because a part of domestic demand falls on foreign goods.

(b) An increase in autonomous demand leads to a smaller increase in output compared to a closed economy.

(c) Under clean floating, the exchange rate is market-determined without any Central bank intervention.

(d) None of the above

↗ *Ans.* *(d)*

Exp. None of the given statement is incorrect regarding External Sector.

The open economy multiplier is smaller than that in a closed economy because a part of domestic demand falls on foreign goods. An increase in autonomous demand leads to a smaller increase in output compared to a closed economy.

It also results in a deterioration of the trade balance. Under clean floating, the exchange rate is market-determined without any Central Bank intervention.

In case of managed floating, Central Bank intervenes to reduce fluctuations in the exchange rate.

24. **In which of the following years, the Indian rupee was devalued twice?** *(Chap 6, Class-XII, New NCERT)*

(a) 1989-90   (b) 1990-91   (c) 1991-92   (d) 1992-93

↗ *Ans.* *(c)*

Exp. In 1991-92, the Indian rupee was devalued twice. It was done to avert the financial crisis and to tackle the issue of Balance of Payment crisis. In 1991, India had a fixed exchange rate system, where the rupee was pegged to the value of a basket of currencies of major trading partners.

This financial crisis led to reforms in foreign exchange management and convertibility of rupee vis-a-vis other currencies. India achieved Current Account Convertibility in August 1994, by accepting Article VIII of the Articles of Agreement of the IMF.

11

Liberalisation, Privatisation and Globalisation

New NCERT Class X (Globalisation and the Indian Economy),
New NCERT Class XI (Liberalisation, Privatisation and Globalisation : An Appraisal)

1. 'Economic Reform' measures in India were formally introduced in

(Chap 3, Class-XI, New NCERT) (WBPSC Pre 2020)

(a) July 1991   (b) August 1947
(c) January 1980   (d) March 1990

↗ *Ans.* (a)

Exp. 'Economic Reform' measures in India were formally introduced in July 1991. This reform was initiated by Indian government on the backdrop of economic crisis relating to balance of payment crisis. This reform also referred as 'New Economic Policy', was responsible for introducing an era of Liberalisation, Privatisation and Globalisation in India.

2. Which of the following statements is incorrect about the Economic Recession of 1991?

(Chap 3, Class-XI, New NCERT)

(a) In 1991, India met with an economic crisis relating to its internal debt.
(b) The government was not able to make repayments on its borrowings from abroad.
(c) Foreign exchange reserves maintained to import petroleum and other important items, dropped to levels that were not sufficient for even a fortnight.
(d) The crisis was further compounded by rising prices of essential goods.

↗ *Ans.* (a)

Exp. Statement (a) is incorrect about the Economic Recession of 1991. In 1991, India met with an economic crisis relating to its external debt (not internal debt) in which government was not able to make repayments on its borrowings from abroad.

Foreign exchange reserves, maintained to import petroleum and other important items, dropped to levels that were not sufficient for even a fortnight. The crisis was further compounded by rising prices of essential goods.

All these led the government to introduce a new set of policy reforms in the country.

3. Which of the following statements regarding New Economic Policy (NEP) is incorrect?

(Chap 3, Class-XI, New NCERT)

(a) The thrust of the NEP was towards creating a more competitive environment in the economy and removing the barriers to entry and growth of firms.
(b) Stabilisation measures are long-term measures, intended to correct some of the weaknesses that have developed in the balance of payments and to bring inflation under control.
(c) Structural reform policies aimed at removing the rigidities in various segments of the Indian economy.
(d) The government initiated a variety of policies, which fall under three heads viz. – Liberalisation, Privatisation and Globalisation.

↗ *Ans.* (b)

Exp. Statement (b) is incorrect regarding New Economic Policy (NEP).

The stabilisation measures introduced as a part of NEP are short-term measures. It intended to correct some of the weaknesses that have developed in the balance of payments and to bring inflation under control.

New Economic Policy was launched in 1991 with the aim to open door for global exposure. In New Economic Policy, government reduced the import duties, opened reserved sector for private players, dwelled Indian currency to increase the export. It is also known as LPG model of growth.

4. Which of the following statements is incorrect about liberalisation? *(Chap 3, Class-XI, New NCERT)*

(a) Industrial licensing was abolished for almost all product categories except alcohol, cigarettes, hazardous chemicals, etc.

(b) The only industries, which are now reserved for the public sector are a part of atomic energy generation and some core activities in railway transport.

(c) Many goods produced by small scale industries have now been de-reserved.

(d) In most industries, the market has not been allowed to determine the prices.

↗ Ans. *(d)*

Exp. Statement (d) is incorrect regarding liberalisation. In liberalisation, the market factors determine the prices of goods and services, on the basis of demand supply.

Liberalisation was introduced as a part of New Economic Policy in 1991 to put an end to restrictions imposed on private capital and open various sectors of the economy. Under this, industrial licensing was abolished for almost all product categories except alcohol, cigarettes and hazardous chemicals.

5. Consider the following statements about liberalisation of financial sector reforms.
(Chap 3, Class-XI, New NCERT)

1. One of the major aims of Financial Sector reforms is to increase the role of RBI as regulator.

2. Foreign Institutional Investors (FII), such as merchant bankers, mutual funds and pension funds, are now allowed to invest in Indian financial markets.

Which of the statement(s) given above is/are incorrect?

(a) Only 1   (b) Only 2
(c) Both 1 and 2   (d) Neither 1 nor 2

↗ Ans. *(a)*

Exp. Statement (1) is incorrect about the liberalisation of financial sector reforms. The financial sector reforms under the liberalisation measure of 1991, envisaged to reduce the role of RBI from regulator to facilitator of Financial Sector. Financial Sector is also allowed to take decisions on many matters without consulting the RBI. FIIs were also allowed with some regulation in financial market.

6. Which of the following is one of the liberalisation policies in the trade and investment policy?
(Chap 3, Class-XI, New NCERT)

(a) Liberalisation of the trade and investment regime was initiated to decrease international competitiveness of industrial production.

(b) Dismantling of quantitative restrictions on imports and exports.

(c) Increase in tariff rates.

(d) Imposition of licensing procedures for imports.

↗ Ans. *(b)*

Exp. Statement (b) is correct.

Dismantling of quantitative restrictions on imports and exports is one of the liberalisation policies in trade and investment policy. Liberalisation of trade and investment regime was initiated to increase international competitiveness of industrial production and also foreign investments and technology into the economy. It also aimed for reduction of tariff rates and removal of licensing procedures for imports.

7. Which of the following statements is incorrect regarding the liberalisation of licensing policy?
(Chap 3, Class-XI, New NCERT)

(a) Import licensing was abolished except in case of hazardous and environmentally sensitive industries.

(b) Qualitative restrictions on imports of manufactured consumer goods and agricultural products were also fully removed from April, 2001.

(c) Export duties have been removed to increase the competitive position of Indian goods in the international markets.

(d) None of the above

↗ Ans. *(b)*

Exp. Statement (b) is incorrect regarding liberalisation of licensing policy as quantitative (not qualitative) restrictions on imports of manufactured consumer goods and agricultural products were also fully removed from April, 2001. Under the trade policy reforms, quantitative restrictions on imports and exports were abolished, tariff rates were reduced, licensing procedures for imports were removed and exports duties were removed to increase the competitive position of Indian goods in the international markets.

8. Which of the following is/are the objective of Privatisation? *(Chap 3, Class XII, New NCERT)*

1. To improve public finance.

2. To reduce the financial burden on the government.

3. To increase the volume of Foreign Direct Investment.

Codes

(a) 1 and 2 (b) 2 and 3
(c) 1, 2 and 3 (d) None of these

↗ **Ans.** (c)

Exp. All the given statements (1), (2) and (3) are correct with regards to the objective of privatisation. Privatisation implies shedding of the ownership or management of a government-owned enterprise.

The objective of privatisation are to reduce the financial burden on the government, to improve public finance, to introduce, competition and market discipline, to depoliticise non-essential services and to encourage a wider share of ownership.

9. **Government companies are converted into private companies in the following ways in India**
(Chap 3, Class XII, New NCERT)

1. By withdrawal of the government from ownership and management of Public Sector Companies.

2. By outright sale of Public Sector Companies.

Which of the statement(s) given above is/are correct?

(a) Only 1 (b) Only 2
(c) Both 1 and 2 (d) Neither 1 nor 2

↗ **Ans.** (c)

Exp. Both the statements (1) and (2) are correct with reference to conversion of government companies to private companies. Government companies are converted into private companies in two ways (i) by withdrawal of the government form ownership and management of Public Sector Companies (PSCs) and (ii) by outright sale of PSCs. Privatisation of PSCs by selling off part of the equity to the public is known as disinvestment.

10. **Which of the following statements is correct with respect to the effects of privatisation?**
(Chap 3, Class-XI, New NCERT)

1. Privatisation could provide strong impetus to the inflow of FDI.

2. Some Public Sector Undertaking (PSUs) have been granted special status as maharatnas, navratnas and miniratnas to ensure autonomy.

Codes

(a) Only 1 (b) Only 2
(c) Both 1 and 2 (d) Neither 1 nor 2

↗ **Ans.** (c)

Exp. Both the given statements are correct with respect to the effects of privatisation. Privatisation implies shedding of ownership or management of a government-owned enterprise. The government

envisaged that privatisation could provide strong impetus to the inflow of Foreign Direct Investment (FDI). Under this measures, some Public Sector Undertakings (PSUs) have been granted special status as maharatnas, navratnas and miniratnas to ensure autonomy.

11. **Identify the correct statement regarding privatisation.** *(Chap 3, Class-XI, New NCERT)*

(a) Government companies are converted into private companies by withdrawal of the government from ownership and management of public sector companies or by outright sale of public sector companies.

(b) The purpose of the sale, according to the government, was mainly to improve financial discipline and facilitate modernisation.

(c) It was also envisaged that private capital and managerial capabilities could be effectively utilised to improve the performance of the PSUs.

(d) All of the above

↗ **Ans.** (d)

Exp. All the given statements are correct regarding privatisation.

Privatisation was introduced as one of the measures in New Economic Policy (NEP) 1991 to increase efficiency and competitiveness of the Indian Public Sector.

It aimed for increasing the productivity and competitiveness of the Indian Public Sector.

For this purpose, Government companies are converted into private companies by withdrawals of the government from ownership and management of public sector. Also, the sale of goods improves the financial discipline and the private capital utilised to improve the performance of the PSUs.

12. **Consider the following statements with respect to privatisation.** *(Chap 3, Class-XI, New NCERT)*

1. It implies shedding of the ownership or management of a government-owned enterprise.

2. Privatisation of the Public Sector Enterprises by selling off part of the equity of PSEs to the public is known as disinvestment.

Which of the statement(s) given above is/are correct?

(a) Only 1 (b) Only 2
(c) Both 1 and 2 (d) Neither 1 nor 2

↗ **Ans.** (c)

Exp. Both the given statements are correct regarding privatisation as it implies shedding of the ownership or management of government-owned enterprises. Government companies are converted into private companies by withdrawal of government ownership and management of public sector companies or by outright sale of public sector companies or privatisation of the Public Sector Enterprises (PSEs) by selling off their equity to the public is known as disinvestment.

13. Consider the following Assertion (A) and Reason (R) and choose the correct code.

(Chap 3, Class-XI, New NCERT)

Assertion (A) Although globalisation is generally understood as integration of the economy of the country with the world economy, but it is a complex phenomenon.

Reason (R) It is an outcome of the set of various policies that are aimed at transforming the World towards greater interdependence and integration.

Codes

(a) Both A and R are true and R is the correct explanation of A.

(b) Both A and R are true, but R is not the correct explanation of A.

(c) A is true, but R is false.

(d) A is false, but R is true.

➤ *Ans.* (a)

Exp. Both Assertion (A) and Reason (R) are correct and Reason (R) is the correct explanation of Assertion (A).

Globalisation implies integration of the economy of the country with the World economy. Simply it means, markets of one country is open for another.

However, it is a complex phenomenon. Also, globalisation is an outcome of the set of various policies involving creation of networks and activities transcending economic, social and geographical boundaries. These policies are aimed at transforming the world towards greater interdependence and integration.

14. Consider the following statements with respect to outsourcing as an outcome of globalisation.

(Chap 3, Class-XI, New NCERT)

1. In outsourcing, a company hires regular service from external sources, mostly from other countries, which was previously provided internally or from within the country.

2. The low wage rates and availability of skilled manpower in India have made it a destination for global outsourcing in the post-reform period.

Which of the statement(s) given above is/are correct?

(a) Only 1 (b) Only 2

(c) Both 1 and 2 (d) Neither 1 nor 2

➤ *Ans.* (c)

Exp. Both the given statements are correct regarding outsourcing as an outcome of globalisation.

In outsourcing, a company hires regular service from external sources, mostly from other countries, which was previously provided internally or from within the country. The growth of Information Technology (IT) has intensified the process of outsourcing.

After the LPG reforms of 1991, most Multinational Corporations (MNCs), and even small companies, are outsourcing their services to India where they can be availed at a cheaper cost with reasonable degree of skill and accuracy.

15. Which one of the following sectors of the Indian economy got the highest growth in the term of GDP contribution after the adoption of LPG model of economic development?

(Chap 3, Class-XI, New NCERT) (BPSC Pre 2016)

(a) Agricultural Sector

(b) Fishing and Forestry Sector

(c) Mining and Quarrying Sector

(d) Services Sector

➤ *Ans.* (d)

Exp. The 'Services Sector' of the Indian economy got the highest growth in the term of GDP contribution after the adoption of LPG model of economic development.

Its contribution to Indian GDP has grown to around 57% and it is the largest recipient of Foreign Direct Investment (FDI) in India.

16. Consider the following statements about the effects of LPG on agriculture.

(Chap 3, Class-XI, New NCERT)

1. Public investment in the agriculture sector especially in infrastructure, which includes irrigation, power, roads, market linkages and research and extension has increased.

2. There has been a shift from production for the domestic market towards production for the export market focusing on cash crops in lieu of production of food grains.

Which of the statement(s) given above is/are incorrect?

(a) Only 1 (b) Only 2

(c) Both 1 and 2 (d) Neither 1 nor 2

➤ *Ans.* (a)

Exp. Statement (1) is incorrect about the effects of LPG on agriculture as after introduction of these reforms, public investment in the agricultural sector especially in infrastructure, which includes irrigation, power, roads, market linkages and research and extension has not increased but decreased. Reforms have not been able to benefit agriculture, where the growth rate has been decelerating.

17. Consider the following statements regarding the LPG reforms in industrial sector.

(Chap 3, Class-XI, New NCERT)

1. Industrial growth has recorded a slowdown because of decreasing demand for industrial products due to various reasons such as cheaper imports, inadequate investment in infrastructure etc.

2. Globalisation is often seen as creating conditions for the free movement of goods and services from foreign countries that adversely affect the local industries and employment opportunities in developing countries.

Which of the statement(s) given above is/are correct?

(a) Only 1 (b) Only 2
(c) Both 1 and 2 (d) Neither 1 nor 2

↗ *Ans.* *(c)*

Exp. Both the given statements are correct regarding the LPG reforms in industrial sector.

Globalisation is often seen as creating conditions for the free movement of goods and services from foreign countries that adversely affect the local industries and employment opportunities in developing countries.

Due to this, domestic manufacturers of India are facing competition from imports.

The slowdown of industrial growth is one of the negative impacts of LPG reforms. It was caused due to decreased demand for industrial products due to various reasons such as cheaper imports, inadequate investment in infrastructure, etc.

18. Which of the following statements is incorrect regarding LPG Reforms and Fiscal Policy?

(Chap 3, Class-XI, New NCERT)

(a) Economic reforms have placed limits on the growth of public expenditure, especially in social sectors.

(b) The tax reductions in the reform period, aimed at yielding larger revenue and curb tax evasion, have not resulted in an increase in tax revenue for the government.

(c) The reform policies involving tariff reduction have increased the scope for raising revenue through custom duties.

(d) In order to attract foreign investment, tax incentives are provided to foreign investors, which further reduces the scope for raising tax revenues.

↗ *Ans.* *(c)*

Exp. Statement (c) is incorrect regarding LPG reforms and Fiscal Policy. One of the negative fallouts of LPG reforms in context of fiscal policies is that, the reform policies involving tariff reduction, have curtailed the scope for raising revenue through custom duties. It has created a negative impact on developmental and welfare expenditures.

19. Which of the following statements is incorrect regarding the criticism of LPG Policy in the Indian economy? *(Chap 3, Class-XI, New NCERT)*

(a) The process of globalisation through liberalisation and privatisation policies has produced positive as well as negative results both for India and other countries.

(b) Globalisation should be seen as an opportunity in terms of greater access to global markets, high technology and increased possibility of large industries of developing countries to become important players in the international arena.

(c) Globalisation is a strategy of developed countries to expand their markets in other countries.

(d) The market-driven globalisation has widened the economic disparities among nations and people.

↗ *Ans.* *(b)*

Exp. Statement (b) is incorrect regarding the criticism of LPG policy in the Indian economy.

Globalisation should be seen as an opportunity in terms of greater access to global markets, high technology and increased possibility for large industries of developing countries, to become important players in the international arena is one of the positive aspects of globalisation. It has integrated the economy of the country with the world economy.

20. Which of the following sector is/are now reserved for the public sector in India?

(Chap 3, Class XII, NCERT)

1. Atomic energy generation.
2. Some core activities in railway.
3. Petroleum products.

Codes

(a) 1 and 2   (b) 2 and 3   (c) 1 and 3   (d) 1, 2 and 3

↗ *Ans.* *(a)*

Exp. Atomic energy generation and some core activities in railway are reserved for the public sector in India.

Due to New Economic policy (NEP) 1991, as of now just two sectors of national importance are reserved for the public enterprises.

The NEPs in India were launched on 24th July, 1991 by then Union Finance Minister Dr. Manmohan Singh and PM PV Narasimha Rao. The main objective of this policy was to open the Indian Economy for the global exposure.

21. Which among the following given factor(s) has/have enabled the process of globalisation?

(Chap 4, Class-X, New NCERT)

1. Increased use of technology
2. Liberalisation of foreign trade and foreign investment policy
3. Removing barriers or restrictions set by the government

Codes

(a) Only 1   (b) 1 and 2
(c) 1, 2 and 3   (d) 1 and 3

↗ *Ans.* *(c)*

Exp. All the given factors have enabled the process of globalisation. Increased use of technology, liberalisation of foreign trade and foreign investment policy and removing barriers or restrictions set by the government are considered as some of the factors that have enabled globalisation.

By these means, globalisation attempts to establish links in such a way that world events influences India and vice-versa.

22. Consider the following Assertion (A) and Reason (R) and choose the correct code.

(Chap 4, Class-X, New NCERT)

Assertion (A) Faced with growing competition, most employers these days prefer to employ workers 'flexibly'.

Reason (R) Globalisation and the pressure of competition have substantially changed the lives of workers.

Codes

(a) Both A and R are true and R is the correct explanation of A.
(b) Both A and R are true, but R is not the correct explanation of A.
(c) A is true, but R is false.
(d) A is false, but R is true.

↗ *Ans.* *(a)*

Exp. Both Assertion (A) and Reason (R) are true and Reason (R) is the correct explanation of Assertion (A). Globalisation and the pressure of competition have substantially changed the lives of workers. Faced with growing competition, most employers these day prefer to employ workers 'flexibly'.

It means that jobs are no longer secure, wages are low and workers have to put in long hours of work. India's employers are facing tough competition and try hard to cut down their cost of production.

23. With reference to the Indian economy after the 1991 economic liberalisation, consider the following statements.

(Chap 3, Class-XI, New NCERT) (IAS Pre 2020)

1. Workers' productivity (₹ per worker at 2004-05 prices) increased in urban areas while it decreased in rural areas.
2. The percentage share of rural areas in the workforce steadily increased.
3. In rural areas, the growth in the non-farm economy increased.
4. The growth rate in rural employment decreased.

Which of the statements given above is/are correct?

(a) 1 and 2   (b) 3 and 4
(c) Only 3   (d) 1, 2 and 4

↗ *Ans.* *(b)*

Exp. Statements (3) and (4) are correct with reference to the Indian economy after the 1991 economic liberalisation.

After the LPG Reforms of 1991, it is inevitable that the rural/agricultural workforce started shifting towards urban/non-agri sectors. With increase in urbanisation and job opportunities, the rural to urban migration took place, which lead to the increase in opportunities in urban areas and decrease in rural areas.

Statements (1) and (2) are incorrect as workers' productivity has increased for both rural and urban areas. With increased urbanisation and more job opportunities in urban areas, the percentage share of rural areas in the workforce has decreased (not increased).

12

International Organisations

Old NCERT Class IX & X (Towards Economic Development), New NCERT Class X (Globalisation and the Indian Economy), New NCERT Class X (Development), New NCERT Class XI (Liberalisation, Privatisation and Globalisation : An Appraisal), New NCERT Class XI (Comparative Development Experiences of Indian and Its Neighbours), New NCERT Class XII (Our Economy : Macroeconomics)

1. Name the United Nation Monetary and Financial Conference wherein the agreements were signed to set up IBRD, GATT and IMF.

(Chap 6, Class-XII, New NCERT) (IAS Pre 2008)

(a) Bandung Conference

(b) Bretton Woods Conference

(c) Versailles Conference

(d) Yalta Conference

↗ *Ans.* (b)

Exp. The United Nation Monetary and Financial Conference wherein the agreements were signed to set up IBRD, GATT and IMF is commonly known as Bretton Woods Conference. This conference was held in July 1944, in New Hampshire, United States.

International Bank for Reconstruction and Development (IBRD) is a part of World Bank group, which provides subsidised loans to least developed and developing countries. The General Agreement on Trade and Tariffs (GATT) is precursor organisation of World Trade Organisation (WTO) specialising in promotion and protection of free trade across the world. The International Monetary Fund (IMF) is responsible for maintaining macroeconomics stability in the world.

2. Bretton Woods Conference led to the establishment of which of the following organisations? *(Chap 6, Class-XII, New NCERT)*

(a) IMF and WTO

(b) World Bank and WTO

(c) IMF and World Bank

(d) WTO and World Economic Forum

↗ *Ans.* (c)

Exp. The Bretton Woods Conference held in 1944 set up the International Monetary Fund (IMF) and World Bank. The World Bank through its highly subsidised loan helps least developed and developing countries to attain economic growth and development. IMF works towards macroeconomic stability and helps countries to meet their shortfall in Balance of Payment.

3. Which of the following statements regarding the World Trade Organisation is correct?

(Chap 4, Class-X, New NCERT)

(a) The WTO was founded in 1948 as the predecessor organisation to the GATT.

(b) GATT was established in 1995 with 3 countries as the global trade organisation to administer all multilateral trade agreements by providing equal opportunities to all countries in the international market for trading purposes.

(c) WTO aims to establish a rule-based trading regime in which nations cannot place arbitrary restrictions on trade.

(d) All of the above

↗ *Ans.* (c)

Exp. Statement (c) is correct regarding the World Trade Organisation as it aims to establish a rule-based trading regime in which nations cannot place arbitrary restrictions on trade.

Statements (a) and (b) are incorrect as the WTO was founded in 1995 as the successor organisation to the GATT (General Agreement on Trade and Tariff).

GATT was established in 1948 with 23 countries as the global trade organisation to administer all multilateral trade agreements by providing equal opportunities to all countries in the international market for trading purpose.

4. **Which of the following statements is correct about the World Trade Organisation (WTO)?**

(Chap 3, Class-XI, New NCERT)

(a) As an important member of WTO, India has been in the forefront of framing fair global rules, regulations and safeguards and advocating the interests of the developing world.

(b) India has kept its commitments towards liberalisation of trade, made in the WTO, by removing quantitative restrictions on imports and reducing tariff rates.

(c) Its purpose is to remove tariff as well as non-tariff barriers and provide greater market access to all member countries.

(d) All of the above

↗ *Ans.* *(d)*

Exp. All the given statements are correct about the WTO. India has been a WTO member since 1st January, 1995. As an important member of WTO, India has been in the forefront of framing fair rules, regulations and safeguards and advocating the interest of developing world. India has kept its commitments towards liberalisation of trade, made in the WTO, by removing quantitative restrictions on imports and reducing tariff rates.

For instance, one of the specific features of Export-Import Policy (2000-01) of India was the removal of quantitative restrictions within the provisions of WTO. The main purpose of WTO is to remove trade barriers and provide greater market access to all member countries.

5. **Consider the following statements about the World Trade Organisation (WTO).**

(Chap 3, Class-XI, New NCERT)

1. Its purpose is also to enlarge production and trade of services, to ensure optimum utilisation of world resources and to protect the environment.

2. The WTO agreements unlike GATT cover trade in goods only.

Which of the statement(s) given above is/are correct?

(a) Only 1   (b) Only 2

(c) Both 1 and 2   (d) Neither 1 nor 2

↗ *Ans.* *(a)*

Exp. Statement (1) is correct about the WTO. Aim of WTO is to liberalise international trade. Its purpose is also to enlarge production and trade of services, to ensure optimum utilisation of world resources and to protect the environment.

Statement (2) is incorrect because the WTO agreements cover trade in goods and services to facilitate international trade (bilateral and multilateral) through removal of tariff as well as non-tariff barriers and providing greater market access to all member countries.

6. **Which of the following statements is incorrect regarding the International Monetary Fund (IMF)?**

(Chap 4, Class-IX & X, Old NCERT)

(a) It is a specialised agency of the United Nations.

(b) It has reserves of currencies of all countries, which are deposited by the respective countries according to their fixed quota.

(c) Unexpected demands for foreign currencies cannot be met through this.

(d) It assists in providing stability in the foreign exchange rates.

↗ *Ans.* *(c)*

Exp. Statement (c) is incorrect regarding the IMF because it assists countries in providing stability in the foreign exchange rates by providing foreign currencies when unexpected demand arises. It also assists countries in case of Balance of Payment Crisis and works towards achieving macroeconomic stability in the world.

International Monetary Fund (IMF) was formed in 1944 at the Bretton Woods Conference, with the goal of restructuring, the International Monetary System. It is the specialised agency of the United Nations (UN). It has reserves of currencies of all countries, which are deposited by the respective countries according to their fixed quota. Nations with greater economic significance have large quotas. It assists in providing stability in the Foreign exchange rates arrangement between countries and allowing their governments to priortise economic growth.

7. **'Gold Tranche' (Reserve Tranche) refers to**

(Chap 4, Class-IX & X, Old NCERT) (IAS Pre 2020)

(a) a loan system of the World Bank.

(b) one of the operations of a Central Bank.

(c) a credit system granted by WTO to its members.

(d) a credit system granted by IMF to its members.

↗ *Ans.* *(d)*

Exp. 'Gold Tranche' (Reserve Tranche) refers to a credit system granted by IMF to its members. It is the component of a member country's quota with the IMF that is in the form of Gold or foreign currency. The funds under Reserve Tranche can be accessed by the countries at any time without service fee or economic reform conditions.

8. **Which of the following statements is correct regarding 'International Monetary Fund'?**

(Chap 6, Class-XII, New NCERT) (MPPSC Pre 2017)

(a) It can grant loans to any country.

(b) It can grant loans to only developed countries.

(c) It grants loans to member countries only in case of Balance of Payments crises.

(d) It grants loans to the Central Bank of a country.

↗ *Ans. (c)*

Exp. Statement (c) is correct regarding International Monetary Fund (IMF). It is an international financial institution specialising in promoting global economic growth and financial stability.

Statements (a), (b) and (d) are incorrect as in case of Balance of Payment (BoP) crisis, it can grant loans to member countries only. It has also created Special Drawing Rights (SDR) as international monetary reserve supplementing the existing money reserves of member countries.

9. **Consider the following statements with respect to International Monetary Fund (IMF).**

(Chap 6, Class-XII, New NCERT)

1. Its calculation of the Special Drawing Rights is based on Euro, Japanese Yen, Dollar, Pound Sterling and Dinar.

2. The original installments of SDRs were distributed to member countries according to their quota in the fund.

Which of the statement(s) given above is/are incorrect?

(a) Only 1   (b) Only 2

(c) Both 1 and 2   (d) Neither 1 nor 2

↗ *Ans. (a)*

Exp. Statement (1) is incorrect with respect to IMF because calculation of Special Drawing Rights (SDR) of IMF is based on weighted sum of five currencies, namely US Dollar, the Euro, the Chinese Renminbi, the Japanese Yen and the British Pound Sterling. It is an international reserve asset created by IMF to supplement the official reserves of its member countries. The original installments of SDRs were distributed to member countries according to their quota in the fund.

10. **Which of the following organisations release the World Development Report?**

(Chap 1, Class-X, New NCERT)

(a) WTO   (b) World Bank

(c) IMF   (d) None of these

↗ *Ans. (b)*

Exp. World Bank releases the World Development Report. It has been published annually since 1978 by World Bank. It is invaluable guide to the economic, social and environmental state of the world today.

The World Bank was created at the Bretton Woods Conference in 1944, as International Bank for Reconstruction and Development. It provides loans and grants to the government of Low and middle income countries for the purpose of pursuing capital projects.

11. **Great Leap Forward (GLF) Campaign and Commune System is related to, which of the following countries?** *(Chap 10, Class-XI, New NCERT)*

(a) India   (b) Pakistan

(c) China   (d) Bangladesh

↗ *Ans. (c)*

Exp. Great Leap Forward (GLF) Campaign and Commune system is related to China.

The Great Leap Forward (GLF) campaign initiated in 1958 aimed at industrialising the country on a massive scale under this campaign. People were encouraged to set up industries in their backyards. In rural areas, communes were started in China. Under the Commune system, people collectively cultivated lands. In 1958, there were 26,000 communes covering all the farm population.

12. **India is a member of which of the following organisations?** *(Glossary, Class XI, New NCERT)*

1. Association of South-East Asian Nations (ASEAN).

2. The South Asian Association for Regional Cooperation (SAARC).

3. G-7

Codes

(a) 1 and 3   (b) 1 and 2

(c) Only 2   (d) 1, 2 and 3

↗ *Ans. (c)*

Exp. India is the member of the South Asian Association for Regional Cooperation (SAARC). It is an association of eight countries of South Asia, namely, Bangladesh, Bhutan, India, Maldives, Nepal, Pakistan, Sri Lanka and Afghanistan. It provides a platform for the peoples of South Asia to work together in a spirit of friendship, trust and understanding.

While India is not the member of ASEAN and G-7.

ASEAN (Association of South-East Asia Nations) is a political, economic and cultural organisation of 10 countries located in South-East Asia. Its members are Brunei, Cambodia, Indonesia, Laos, Malaysia, Myanmar, the Philippines, Singapore, Thailand and Vietnam. Also G-7 (Group-7) is an association of most developed 7 countries of the world. Its current members are France, Germany, Italy, Japan, the US, the UK and Canada.

13. Which of the following countries is not a member of the European Union? *(Glossary, Class-X, New NCERT)*

(a) France (b) Lithuania
(c) Germany (d) Russia

↗ *Ans.* *(d)*

Exp. Russia is not a member of the European Union. European Union is a union of 27 member states that are located primarily in Europe. It was founded to enhance political, economic and social cooperation within the European continent.

The member states of European Union are Austria, Belgium, Bulgaria, Croatia, Cyprus, Czech Republic, Denmark, Estonia, Finland, France, Germany, Greece, Hungary, Ireland, Italy, Latvia, Lithuania, Luxembourg, Malta, Netherlands, Poland, Portugal, Romania, Slovakia, Slovenia, Spain and Sweden.

14. Which of the following is not associated with NAFTA? *(Chap 9, Class-XII, New NCERT) (BPSC Pre 2018)*

(a) Great Britain (b) Canada
(c) Mexico (d) USA

↗ *Ans.* *(a)*

Exp. Great Britain is not associated with the North American Free Trade Association (NAFTA). It is a multilateral trading organisation founded by United States, Canada and Mexico in 1994. It is one of the largest trade blocs in the world in terms of gross domestic product. On 1st July, 2020, NAFTA was replaced by US-Mexico-Canada Agreement (USMCA).

15. Consider the following statements with respect to SAARC. *(Glossary, Class-XI, New NCERT)*

1. It comprises of seven South Asian countries.
2. The main objectives of SAARC is social and economic development of the member countries.

Which of the statement(s) given above is/are correct?

(a) Only 1 (b) Only 2
(c) Both 1 and 2 (d) Neither 1 nor 2

↗ *Ans.* *(b)*

Exp. Statement (2) is correct with respect to South Asian Association for Regional Corporation (SAARC). SAARC is an association of eight countries of South Asia—Bangladesh, Bhutan, India, Maldives, Nepal, Pakistan, Sri Lanka and Afghanistan.

It aims to accelerate the process of economic and social development in member countries. It was established in 1985 and headquartered in Kathmandu (Nepal).

16. Which of the following statements is incorrect about G-20? *(Glossary, Class-XI, New NCERT)*

(a) It works to promote international financial stability and sustainable development.
(b) India is a member nation of G-20.
(c) The European Union is not a member of this organisation.
(d) All of the above

↗ *Ans.* *(c)*

Exp. Statement (c) is incorrect about G-20 because the European Union is the member of G-20. It is represented by the President of the European Council and head of European Central Bank.

G-20 is a forum of countries that intents to promote global economic stability and sustainable growth.

India is also the member of G-20. The other members of G-20 besides India and European Union are Argentina, Australia, Brazil, Japan, South Korea, Mexico, Russia, Saudi Arabia, South Africa, Turkey, United Kingdom, USA, Canada, China, France, Germany, Indonesia, Italy.

PRACTICE SETS

Practice Set 1

1. Consider the following statements. *(IAS Pre 2021)*

1. The Governor of the Reserve Bank of India (RBI) is appointed by the Central Government.
2. Certain provisions in the Constitution of India provide the Central Government the right to issue directions to the RBI in public interest.
3. The Governor of the RBI draws his power from the RBI Act.

Which of the statements given above are correct?

(a) 1 and 2   (b) 2 and 3
(c) 1 and 3   (d) 1, 2 and 3

2. The money multiplier in an economy increases with, which one of the following? *(IAS Pre 2021)*

(a) Increase in the Cash Reserve Ratio in the banks.
(b) Increase in the Statutory Liquidity Ratio in the banks.
(c) Increase in the banking habits of the people.
(d) Increase in the population of the country.

3. In India, the central bank's function as the 'lender of last resort' usually refers to, which of the following? *(IAS Pre 2021)*

1. Lending to trade and industry bodies when they fail to borrow from other sources.
2. Providing liquidity to the banks having a temporary crisis.
3. Lending to governments to finance budgetary deficits.

Codes

(a) 1 and 2   (b) Only 2   (c) 2 and 3   (d) Only 3

4. With reference to 'Urban Cooperative Banks' in India, consider the following statements.

(IAS Pre 2021)

1. They are supervised and regulated by local boards set up by the State Governments.
2. They can issue equity shares and preference shares.
3. They were brought under the purview of the Banking Regulation Act, 1949 through an Amendment in 1966.

Which of the statements given above is/are correct?
(a) Only 1   (b) 2 and 3
(c) 1 and 3   (d) 1, 2 and 3

5. With reference to India, consider the following statements. *(IAS Pre 2021)*

1. Retail investors through demat account can invest in 'Treasury Bills' and 'Government of India Debt Bonds' in primary market.
2. The 'Negotiated Dealing System-Order Matching' is a government securities trading platform of the Reserve Bank of India.
3. The 'Central Depository Services Ltd.' is jointly promoted by the Reserve Bank of India and the Bombay Stock Exchange.

Which of the statements given above is/are correct?
(a) Only 1   (b) 1 and 2
(c) Only 3   (d) 2 and 3

6. Which of the following measures would result in an increase in the money supply in the economy? *(IAS Pre 2012)*

1. Purchase of government securities from the public by the Central Bank.
2. Deposit of currency in commercial banks by the public.
3. Borrowing by the government from the Central Bank.
4. Sale of government securities to the public by the Central Bank.

Codes

(a) Only 1   (b) 2 and 4
(c) 1 and 3   (d) 2, 3 and 4

7. Which of the following statement(s) is/are correct about pension schemes in India?

1. Atal Pension Yojana is operated by department of Finance services.
2. There is no minimum or maximum income limit to join Atal Pension Scheme.

3. Unorganised sector workers with monthly income upto fifteen thousand can only join Pradhan Mantri Shram yogi Maandhan yojna.

4. Ministry of Labour and Employment operates Pradhan Mantri Shram Yogi Maandhan Yojana.

Codes

(a) Only 1   (b) 1, 2 and 3

(c) Only 4   (d) All of these

8. Consider the following statements.

1. Progressive taxation takes large percentage of tax from high income individuals.

2. Capital gain tax is a direct tax.

3. Surcharge is considered as tax on tax.

Which of the statement(s) given above is/are correct?

(a) Only 3   (b) 1 and 3

(c) All of these   (d) None of these

9. Consider the following statements.

1. Interest for Marginal Standing facility is Repo rate plus 1%.

2. Prompt corrective action are quantitative tools of RBI.

Which of the statement(s) given above is/are incorrect?

(a) Only 1   (b) Only 2

(c) Both 1 and 2   (d) None of these

10. Consider the following statements regarding Indian planning.   *(IAS Pre 2009)*

1. The Second Five-year Plan emphasised on the establishment of heavy industries.

2. The Third Five-year Plan introduced the concept of import substitution as a strategy for industrialisation.

Which of the statements given above is/are correct?

(a) Only 1   (b) Only 2

(c) Both 1 and 2   (d) Neither 1 nor 2

11. Consider the following statements.

1. Mining is a primary sector activity.

2. Uber is an example of Gig economy.

3. Poultry farming is a secondary sector activity.

4. A doctor in India advising patient of Dubai, is an example of Service exports.

Which of the statement(s) given above is/are correct?

(a) 1 and 2   (b) 2 and 3

(c) 1, 2 and 4   (d) 1, 2 and 3

12. Choose the incorrectly matched pair.

(a) Demand Liabilities – Fixed deposits

(b) Time Liabilities – Current deposits

(c) Imperial Bank of India – SBI

(d) Urjit Patel Committee – MSME

13. Post-liberalisation, the government's role has been reduced in the economy. In which of the following sectors, the government does not play a major role as an investor?

(a) Education   (b) Health

(c) Social security   (d) Real estate

14. Which is not the purpose of forming Banks Board Bureau?

1. The bureau will recommend appointment of senior officials in public-sector banks from government interference.

2. The bureau will inspect the level of NPAs of public-sector banks.

3. The bureau will identify the best practices in private-sector banks and seek their implementation in public sector banks.

Codes

(a) Only 1   (b) 2 and 3

(c) 1 and 2   (d) 1, 2 and 3

15. The difference between a bank and a non-banking financial institution (NBFI) is that

(a) A bank interacts directly with customers, while an NBFI interacts with banks and governments.

(b) A bank indulges in a number of activities relating to finance with a range of customers, while an NBFI is mainly concerned with the term loan needs of customers.

(c) A bank deals with both internal and international customers, while an NBFI is mainly concerned with the finances of foreign companies.

(d) A bank's main interest is to help in business transactions and savings/investment activities, while an NBFI's main interest is in the stabilisation of the currency.

16. What is money laundering?

(a) Money laundering is the process of transferring foreign currency abroad.

(b) Money laundering is the process of concealing the source of money.

(c) Money laundering is the process of transferring money to support illegal activities.

(d) Money laundering is the process of transferring money from tax havens.

17. What is the objective of introducing General Anti-Avoidance Rule (GAAR)?

(a) GAAR aims at introducing administrative mechanism to deal with illegal exchange of foreign currency.

(b) GAAR are rules to prevent tax avoidance by multinational companies.

(c) GAAR are rules to prevent transfer of money through hawala system.

(d) None of the above

18. Consider the following statements.

1. More than 55% of the people in India are directly or indirectly dependent on agriculture.
2. Industrial sector contributes 33% in India's GDP.
3. Dairy and Poultry sector contributes 11% to GDP of India.

Which of the statement(s) given above is/are correct?

(a) Only 3　　　　　(b) 2 and 3
(c) All of these　　　(d) None of these

19. Consider the following statements and identify correct ones.

1. Reduction in Repo rate increase money multiplier.
2. Reduction in Case Reserve Ratio By RBI indicates less Risk awaited assets with banks.

Codes

(a) Only 1
(b) Only 2
(c) Both 1 and 2
(d) None of the above

20. Which of the following statement is correct?

(a) Indonesia is not a member of G20 countries.

(b) India is largest exporter of vegetable oil in the world.

(c) Palm oil is used in cosmetic industries.

(d) South Africa is the largest importer of Indian Mangoes.

21. Devaluation of a currency means

(a) Reduction in the value of a currency vis a vis major internationally traded currencies.

(b) Permitting the currency to seek its worth in the international market.

(c) Fixing the value of the currency in conjunction with the movement in the value of a basket of predetermined currencies.

(d) Fixing the value of a currency in multilateral consultation with the IMF, the World Bank and major trading partners.

22. Which of the following statement(s) is/are correct?

1. Whole Sale Price Index measure the change in the price of goods sold and traded in Bulk.
2. Consumer Price Index is calculated by Office of Economic Advisor.

Codes

(a) Only 1
(b) Only 2
(c) Both 1 and 2
(d) None of the above

23. Capital account convertibility of the Indian rupee implies

(a) That the Indian rupee can be exchanged by authorised dealers for travel.

(b) That the Indian rupee can be exchanged for any major currency for the purpose of trade in goods and services.

(c) That the Indian rupee can be exchanged for any major currency for the purpose of trading in financial assets.

(d) None of the above

24. Match List I with List II and select the correct answer using the codes given below.

	List I		List II
A.	WTO	1.	Provides loans to address short-term balance of payment problems
B.	IDA	2.	Multilateral trade negotiation body
C.	IMF	3.	Sanction of soft loans
D.	IBRD	4.	Facilitating lending and borrows for reconstruction and development

Codes

	A	B	C	D			A	B	C	D
(a)	1	2	3	4		(b)	2	1	4	3
(c)	4	3	2	1		(d)	2	1	3	4

25. Which of the following statement is incorrect?

(a) Balance of Payment is a systematic statement of all economic transactions of a country with the rest of the world.

(b) Gold reserves with RBI are not part of Forex reserves.

(c) Increase in inflation rate can increase the demand for foreign currency.

(d) Rate at which one country's currency exchanges for a basket of multiple foreign currencies is Nominal Exchange Rate.

26. Consider the following statements regarding post-liberalisation India's balance of payments position.

1. The current account deficit is on account of net import of services.
2. The capital account surplus is on account of large amount of external assistance received on bilateral basis.
3. The balance of payments situation has improved post-liberalisation.

Which of the statement(s) given above is/are correct?

(a) Only 3   (b) 2 and 3
(c) 1 and 2   (d) 1 and 3

27. Which of the following pair is incorrectly matched?

(a) Darpan portal – NITI Aayog
(b) POSHAN Abhiyan – Ministry of Women and development
(c) Base year for Consumer price Index – 2015
(d) SAUBHAGYA Scheme – Ministry of Power

28. Consider the following statements.

1. Samarth Udyog Bharat 4.0 aims to promote technological solutions to Indian manufacturing units to make them ready for industry 4.0 by 2025.
2. Recovery and Recycling is a part of Circular economic model.
3. National policy on electronics targets $400 from electronic manufacturing by 2025.

Which of the statement(s) given above is/are correct?

(a) Only 1   (b) 2 and 3
(c) All of these   (d) None of these

29. Which of the following statements is/are correct regarding FDI under automatic route?

1. FDI in India under the automatic route does not require prior approval either by the Government of India or the Reserve Bank of India.
2. Investors are only required to notify the concerned regional office of the RBI before receipt of inward remittances and file required documents with the office before the issue of shares to foreign investors.

Codes

(a) Only 1   (b) Only 2
(c) Both 1 and 2   (d) Neither 1 nor 2

30. Which of the following statement is not true?

(a) The World Trade Organisation (WTO) requires member nations to give national treatment to international goods and services.
(b) The General Agreement on Tariffs and Trade (GATT) was replaced by the World Trade Organisation (WTO) in 1995.
(c) The most favoured nation principle under GATT provided that preferential trading agreements reached with one country should be extended to other countries.
(d) The WTO has been able to cover in its agreements the direct taxation policies of member nations.

Practice Set 2

1. With reference to Indian economy, demand pull-inflation can be caused/increased by which of the following? *(IAS Pre 2021)*
   1. Expansionary policies
   2. Fiscal stimulus
   3. Inflation-indexing wages
   4. Higher – purchasing power
   5. Rising interest rates

   Codes
   (a) 1, 2 and 4
   (b) 3, 4 and 5
   (c) 1, 2, 3 and 5
   (d) 1, 2, 3, 4 and 5

2. With reference to the casual workers employed in India, consider the following statements. *(IAS Pre 2021)*
   1. All casual workers are entitled for Employees Provident Fund coverage.
   2. All casual workers are entitled for regular working hours and overtime payment.
   3. The government can by a notification specify that an establishment or industry shall pay wages only through its bank account.

   Which of the statements given above are correct?
   (a) 1 and 2
   (b) 2 and 3
   (c) 1 and 3
   (d) 1, 2 and 3

3. Which among the following steps is most likely to be taken at the time of an economic recession? *(IAS Pre 2021)*
   (a) Cut in tax rates accompanied by increase in interest rate.
   (b) Increase in expenditure on public projects.
   (c) Increase in tax rates accompanied by reduction of interest rate.
   (d) Reduction of expenditure on public projects.

4. Which one of the following is likely to be the most inflationary in its effects? *(IAS Pre 2021)*
   (a) Repayment of Public debt.
   (b) Borrowing from the public to finance a budget deficit.
   (c) Borrowing from the banks to finance a budget deficit.
   (d) Creation of new money to finance a budget deficit.

5. Other things remaining unchanged, market demand for a good might increase if *(IAS Pre 2021)*
   1. Price of its substitute increases.
   2. Price of its complement increases.
   3. The good is an inferior good and income of the consumers increases.
   4. Its price falls.

   Which of the statements given above are correct?
   (a) 1 and 4 (b) 2, 3 and 4
   (c) 1, 3 and 4 (d) 1, 2 and 3

6. Consider the following.
   1. Currency with the public
   2. Demand deposits with banks
   3. Time deposits with banks

   Which of the following above are included in Broad Money (M3)?
   (a) 1 and 2 (b) 1 and 3
   (c) 2 and 3 (d) 1, 2 and 3

7. Consider the following statements.
   1. Near money is an asset that is highly liquid and can be readily converted into cash.
   2. A promissory note is legal financial tool declared by a party promising another to pay the debt on a particular day.

   Which of the statement(s) given above is/are correct?
   (a) Only 1 (b) Only 2
   (c) Both 1 and 2 (d) Neither 1 nor 2

8. Consider the following statements.

1. Sujit Bhalla committee suggested the government to issue Elephant Bonds.
2. Elephant bonds are an instrument to recover black money.

Which of the statement(s) given above is/are correct?

(a) Only 1
(b) Only 2
(c) Neither 1 nor 2
(d) Both 1 and 2

9. Which of the following statement(s) is/are correct?

1. Indian Renewable Energy Development Agency (IREDA) launched India's first Masala bond at London Stock exchange.
2. Seychelles issued world's first 'Blue Bond'.
3. Paid up capital is amount paid by shareholders for the share held by them in company.

Codes

(a) Only 3
(b) Only 1
(c) All of these
(d) 1 and 2

10. Which of the following statement is/are incorrect?

1. Venture capital is a type of private equity use to finance emerging firms that have growth potential.
2. Insurance companies are liability driven financial intermediaries.

Codes

(a) Only 1
(b) Only 2
(c) Both 1 and 2
(d) Neither 1 nor 2

11. Consider the following statements.

1. NIRVIC is an Export Credit Insurance Scheme operated by Ministry of Commerce through Export Credit Guarantee Corporation (ECGC).
2. Motor Vehicle Act 1988 requires all motor vehicle owners to purchase third party insurance.

Which of the statement(s) given above is/are correct?

(a) Only 1
(b) Only 2
(c) Both 1 and 2
(d) Neither 1 nor 2

12. Consider the following statements.

1. Post office saving banks were formed under government saving bank act 1873.
2. India post payment bank are registered under Companies act 2013.

Which of the statement(s) given above is/are correct?

(a) Only 1
(b) Only 2
(c) Both 1 and 2
(d) Neither 1 nor 2

13. Consider the following statements.

1. Sukanya Samridhi scheme focuses on encouraging the parents of girl child for building fund for the education and marriage expenses of her.
2. Mudra Unit development and refinery agency is 100% subsidiary of SBI.

Which of the statement(s) given above is/are correct?

(a) Only 1
(b) Only 2
(c) Both 1 and 2
(d) Neither 1 nor 2

14. Which of the statements given below are incorrect?

1. Excise duty is part of GST.
2. FDI involves setting up firms to produce goods and services.
3. The share of Direct tax is always more than indirect tax in India.

Codes

(a) 1 and 2
(b) 2 and 3
(c) All of these
(d) 1 and 3

15. Identify the incorrectly matched pair.

(a) Bretton Wood Conference – IMF
(b) International bank for reconstruction and development – World Bank
(c) Global economic prospect report – Asian Development Bank
(d) New development Bank – BRICS

16. Which of the following statement is correct?

(a) Short term fixed income instruments like promissory notes are traded in money market.
(b) RN Malhotra Committee in 1993 was constituted for reform in Money market.
(c) Bond is equity instrument.
(d) India currently accounts for 3% of the world's total insurance premium and 5% of the world's life insurance.

17. Which of the following statement is correct?

(a) India is not a member of International Center For Settlement of Investment Disputes (ICSID).
(b) Remittance report is a biannual report by IMF.
(c) Global Tranche Credit system is a tool of WTO.
(d) World Economic outlook report is released by World Bank.

18. **Which of the following statement is incorrect?**

(a) Bottleneck inflation takes place when the supply falls drastically and the demand remains at the same level

(b) Philip Curve advocates a relation between inflation and unemployment in an economy.

(c) A shortfall in total spending of the government over the national income creates deflationary gap in economy.

(d) An inflation for a short period is called core inflation.

19. **Which among the following is added to the gross domestic product to arrive at national income of a nation?**

1. Depreciation
2. Subsidies
3. Indirect taxes
4. Net factor income abroad

Codes

(a) Only 2   (b) 1 and 2   (c) 2 and 3   (d) 3 and 4

20. **Which of the following statements is/are incorrect?**

1. KAPILA program is launched to increase Intellectual property related literacy among people.
2. Global intellectual property index is launched by World bank.

Codes

(a) Only 1   (b) Only 2

(c) Both 1 and 2   (d) Neither 1 nor 2

21. **Human capital formation as a concept is better explained in terms of a process which enables**

(IAS Pre 2018)

1. Individuals of a country to accumulate more capital.
2. Increasing the knowledge, skill levels and capacities of the people of the country.
3. Accumulation of tangible wealth.
4. Accumulation of intangible wealth.

Which of the statements given above is/are correct?

(a) 1 and 2   (b) Only 2

(c) 2 and 4   (d) 1, 3 and 4

22. **With reference to digital payments, consider the following statements.** *(IAS Pre 2018)*

1. BHIM app allows the user to transfer money to anyone with a UPI-enabled bank account.
2. While a chip-pin debit card has four factors of authentication, BHIM app has only two factors of authentication.

Which of the statements given above is/are correct?

(a) Only 1   (b) Only 2

(c) Both 1 and 2   (d) Neither 1 nor 2

23. **Consider the following statements.**

1. The Fiscal Responsibility and Budget Management (FRBM) Review Committee Report has recommended a debt to GDP ratio of 60% for the general (combined) government by 2023, comprising 40% for the Central Government and 20% for the State Governments.
2. The Central Government has domestic liabilities of 21% of GDP as compared to that of 49% of GDP of the State Governments.
3. As per the Constitution of India, it is mandatory for a State to take the Central Government's consent for raising any loan, if the former owes any outstanding liabilities to the latter.

Which of the statements given above is/are correct?

(a) Only 1   (b) 2 and 3   (c) 1 and 3   (d) 1, 2 and 3

24. **Consider the following statements.**

1. Har Khet ko Pani is an initiative under Pradhanmantri Sinchai Yojana.
2. Neeranchal is a watershed program assisted by World Bank.
3. No chemical fertiliser is used in Organic Farming.

Which of the statements given above are correct?

(a) 1 and 2   (b) 2 and 3

(c) 1 and 3   (d) 1, 2 and 3

25. **Consider the following statements.**

1. Financial intermediaries are entity that acts as the middleman between two parties in a financial transaction
2. Building societies, hire purchase companies, insurance companies, saving banks, pension funds, investment trusts are example of non-banking financial Intermediaries

Which of the statements given above is/are incorrect?

(a) Only 1   (b) Only 2

(c) Both 1 and 2   (d) Neither 1 nor 2

26. **Consider the following statements.** *(IAS Pre 2017)*

1. National Payments Corporation of India (NPCI) helps in promoting the financial inclusion in the country.
2. NPCI has launched Rupay, a card payment scheme.

Which of the statements given above is/are correct?

(a) Only 1   (b) Only 2

(c) Both 1 and 2   (d) Neither 1 nor 2

27. Which of the following pair is incorrectly matched?

(a) Delhi-Mumbai Industrial Corridor (DMIC) – Japan

(b) Chennai-Bengaluru Industrial Corridor (CBIC) – Japan

(c) Bengaluru-Mumbai Economic Corridor (BMEC) – World Bank

(d) East Coast Economic Corridor (ECEC) – Asian Development Bank

28. Consider the following statements and choose the correct answer.

1. Under Antyodya Anna Yojana poorest households will receive 35 kg of grain per month.

2. Government announces Minimum Support Price (MSP) for 24 crops.

Codes

(a) Only 1

(b) Both 1 and 2

(c) Only 2

(d) Neither 1 nor 2

29. Consider the following statements.

1. Special Economic Zones (SEZ) in India are operated by the Ministry of industries and public sector undertakings.

2. Invest India program is the official investment promotion and facilitates investments in the country.

Which of the statement(s) given above is/are correct?

(a) Only 1   (b) Both 1 and 2

(c) Only 2   (d) Neither 1 nor 2

30. Consider the following statements.

1. Under monetary policy framework RBI will be responsible for containing inflation targets at 4%, with standard deviation of 2%.

2. Cooperative banks function on the basis of no-profit no-loss.

Which of the statements given above is/are incorrect?

(a) Only 1   (b) Both 1 and 2

(c) Only 2   (d) Neither 1 nor 2

Practice Set 3

1. The effect of devaluation of a currency is that it necessarily: *(IAS Pre 2021)*
1. Improves the competitiveness of the domestic exports in the foreign markets.
2. Increases the foreign value of domestic currency.
3. Improves the trade balance.

Which of the statement(s) given above is/are correct?
(a) Only 1   (b) 1 and 2
(c) Only 3   (d) 2 and 3

2. Indian Government Bond Yields are influenced by which of the following? *(IAS Pre 2021)*
1. Actions of the United States Federal Reserve.
2. Actions of the Reserve Bank of India.
3. Inflation and short-term interest rates.

Which of the statement(s) given above is/are correct?
(a) 1 and 2   (b) Only 2
(c) Only 3   (d) 1, 2 and 3

3. Consider the following statements. *(IAS Pre 2021)*
1. Foreign Currency Convertible Bonds.
2. Foreign Institutional investment with certain conditions.
3. Global depository receipts (GDR).
4. Non-resident external deposits.

Which of the above can be included in Foreign Direct Investments?
(a) 1, 2 and 3   (b) Only 3
(c) 2 and 4   (d) 1 and 4

4. Consider the following statements.
1. The Reserve Bank of India decides the extent of borrowings permitted to the Government of India.
2. The borrowing programme of the Government of India is administered by the Department of Revenue, Ministry of Finance.

Which of the statement(s) given above is/are correct?
(a) Only 1   (b) Only 2
(c) Both 1 and 2   (d) Neither 1 nor 2

5. In the context of Indian economy, 'open' market operations' refer to *(IAS Pre 2013)*
(a) Borrowing by scheduled banks from the RBI.
(b) Lending by commercial banks to industry and trade.
(c) Purchase and sale of government securities by the RBI.
(d) None of the above

6. Consider the following statements.
1. A capital budget is associated with income and expenditure that are of long term nature.
2. Selling of Public Sector units is an example of revenue receipts.
3. Repo rate is increased by RBI after every budget.

Which of the statement(s) given above is/are correct?
(a) Only 1   (b) Only 2
(c) Both 1 and 2   (d) None of these

7. Consider the following statements.
1. The Wholesale Price Index gives more weightage to the primary products because of the dominant role of agriculture in the Indian economy.
2. The Consumer Price Index gives more weightage to manufactured articles on account of change in demand pattern in the economy.

Which of the statements given above is/are correct?
(a) Only 1   (b) Only 2
(c) Both 1 and 2   (d) Neither 1 nor 2

8. Which of the following statement(s) is/are correct?
1. Commercial banks have to compulsorily lend 40% to priority sectors.
2. Startups are included in priority sector lending.
3. Scheduled Commercial banks are the ones listed in Second Schedule of RBI.

Codes
(a) 1 and 2   (b) Only 3
(c) All of these   (d) 2 and 3

9. **Which of the following statement is incorrect?**
(a) Expansionary monetary policy used to decrease money supply.
(b) Monetary Policy Committee is a statutory body.
(c) Monetary Policy Committee decides the benchmark interest rate.
(d) Financial stability and development council constituted after recommendation of Raghuram Rajan Committee.

10. **Consider the following statements.**
1. MCLR is the minimum interest rate of a bank below, which it cannot lend.
2. Ways and means advances are temporary loan facilities to the Centre and State Government.

Which of the statement(s) given above is/are correct?
(a) Both 1 and 2   (b) None of these
(c) Only 2   (d) Only 1

11. **Which of the following pair is incorrectly matched?**

Organisations	Foundation year
(a) EPFO	1952
(b) SEBI	1992
(c) IRDAI	1999
(d) NABARD	1984

12. **Budget deficit may lead to**
1. Rise in the interest rates
2. Fall in value of currency
3. Increase in currency circulation

Which of the statements given above is/are correct?
(a) 1 and 2
(b) 1, 2 and 3
(c) 1 and 3
(d) 2 and 3

13. **Consider the following statements.**
1. India's net exports of goods have a negative balance.
2. India's net export of services have a positive balance.
3. India is the largest receiver of remittances around the world.

Which of the statement(s) given above is/are correct?
(a) Only 2   (b) 2 and 3
(c) 1 and 2   (d) 1, 2 and 3

14. **Consider the following statements.**
1. Short term debt instruments are usually 'unsecured' because they are not backed by any asset.
2. Masala bonds are rupee dominated bonds released in domestic market.

Which of the statement(s) given above is/are correct?
(a) Only 1   (b) Only 2
(c) Both 1 and 2   (d) None of these

15. **Which of the following pair is incorrectly matched?**
(a) Fitch – Rating Agency
(b) Nationalisation of 14 private sector banks – 1991
(c) Basel Norms – Banking
(d) Panda Bonds – Chinese Yen Dominated Bonds

16. **Consider the following statements.**
1. Jan Arogya Yojana is a free health insurance cover upto 2 Lakh for old persons.
2. National Health authority oversees and monitors the implementation of PM-JAY.

Which of the statement(s) given above is/are incorrect?
(a) Only 1   (b) Only 2
(c) All of these   (d) None of these

17. **Which of the following statement is incorrect?**
1. Contractionary fiscal policy involves rising taxes or cutting government spending.
2. Tax cut is a feature of expansionary fiscal policy.
3. Budget is an annual financial statement under Article 110 of Constitution.
4. In 1887 British Indian Government started financial year from 1st April to 31st March.

Codes
(a) Only 1   (b) 3 and 4
(c) 1 and 2   (d) All of these

18. **Consider the following statements.**
1. Increase in revenue expenditure may lead to inflation.
2. Capital expenditure will not have any impact on employment generation.
3. Interest received on loans is a part of revenue receipts.

Which of the statement(s) given above is/are correct?
(a) Only 1   (b) 1 and 2
(c) 1 and 3   (d) All of these

19. Which of the following statement(s) is/are correct?
1. Nauru is the last country to join World Bank.
2. International Center for Settlement of Investment Disputes (ICSID) works under IMF.

Codes
(a) Only 1 (b) Both 1 and 2
(c) Only 2 (d) None of these

20. Which of the following pair is correctly matched?
(a) Trade and development report – World Economic Forum
(b) Marrakesh Agreement – WTO
(c) ILO – Founded in 1939
(d) World Social Prospect Report – UNICEF

21. Which of the following statement(s) is/are correct?
1. World Economic Forum is a non-profitable foundation.
2. Great reset initiative in the post Covid world is launched by World Economic Forum.
3. India is a member of G7 countries.

Codes
(a) Only 1
(b) All of the above
(c) 1 and 2
(d) Only 3

22. In India, which of the following review the independent regulators in sectors like telecommunications, insurance, electricity etc?
(IAS Pre 2019)
1. Ad Hoc Committees set up by the Parliament.
2. Parliamentary Department Related Standing Committees
3. Finance Commission
4. Financial Sector Legislative Reforms Commission
5. NITI Aayog.

Codes
(a) 1 and 2
(b) 1, 3 and 4
(c) 3, 4 and 5
(d) 2 and 5

23. Priority-Sector lending by banks in India constitutes lending to
(a) Agriculture
(b) Micro and small enterprises
(c) Weaker sections
(d) All of the above

24. Consider the following statements.
1. In floating exchange rate, market forces determines the value of domestic currency.
2. Sterlisation by RBI is the process by which RBI takes away access liquidity from banking system to neutralise the fresh money that enter the market.

Which of the statement(s) given above is/are correct?
(a) Only 1 (b) Both 1 and 2
(c) Only 2 (d) Neither 1 nor 2

25. Which of the following statement(s) is/are correct?
1. Exports increases if rupee depreciates.
2. Government of India decides the exchange rate for rupee.

Codes
(a) Only 1 (b) Only 2
(c) Both 1 and 2 (d) Neither 1 nor 2

26. Which of the following statement(s) is/are incorrect?
1. A micro enterprise is the one in which investment does not exceed 1cr and turn over not more than 5cr.
2. Udayam Sakhi Portal has been launched for women entrepreneurs.

Codes
(a) Only 1 (b) Both 1 and 2
(c) Only 2 (d) Neither 1 nor 2

27. Consider the following statements.
1. Monetary Policy Committee uses WPI data to control Inflation.
2. National Statistical Office (NSO) releases WPI.
3. An MBA working in BPO is an example of Disguised Unemployment.

Which of the statement(s) given above is/are correct?
(a) Only 3
(b) 2 and 3
(c) 1, 2 and 3
(d) None of the above

28. Consider the following statements.
1. Open market operation refers to purchase and sale of Government securities by RBI.
2. Call Money market is an Interbank money market for short term financial assets.
3. Market stabilisation Scheme is a policy tool of RBI to suck excess liquidity from the market.

Which of the statement(s) given above is/are correct?
(a) Only 1   (b) 1 and 3
(c) 2 and 3   (d) All of these

29. Which of the following services are accounted in the gross domestic product of a country?
1. Services rendered by a domestic help.
2. Services rendered by a worker from unorganised sector.
3. Services produced in Indian embassies located abroad.
4. Services produced in foreign military establishments located in India.

Codes
(a) 1 and 2   (b) 1, 2 and 3
(c) 2, 3 and 4   (d) 1, 2, 3 and 4

30. Which of the following are responsible for the decrease in per capita holding of cultivated land in India?
1. Low per capita income.
2. Rapid rate of increase in population.
3. Practice of dividing land among the heirs.
4. Use of traditional techniques of ploughing.

Codes
(a) 1 and 2   (b) 2 and 3
(c) 1 and 4   (d) 2, 3 and 4

Answers

▪ Practice Set 1

1. (c)	2. (c)	3. (b)	4. (b)	5. (b)	6. (c)	7. (d)	8. (c)	9. (b)	10. (d)
11. (c)	12. (d)	13. (c)	14. (b)	15. (c)	16. (b)	17. (c)	18. (d)	19. (c)	20. (c)
21. (b)	22. (a)	23. (a)	24. (d)	25. (b)	26. (c)	27. (c)	28. (c)	29. (d)	30. (a)

▪ Practice Set 2

1. (a)	2. (d)	3. (b)	4. (d)	5. (a)	6. (d)	7. (c)	8. (d)	9. (c)	10. (d)
11. (c)	12. (d)	13. (a)	14. (d)	15. (c)	16. (a)	17. (a)	18. (d)	19. (c)	20. (b)
21. (a)	22. (a)	23. (c)	24. (a)	25. (c)	26. (c)	27. (c)	28. (b)	29. (c)	30. (d)

▪ Practice Set 3

1. (a)	2. (b)	3. (a)	4. (d)	5. (c)	6. (a)	7. (a)	8. (c)	9. (a)	10. (a)
11. (d)	12. (a)	13. (b)	14. (a)	15. (b)	16. (a)	17. (b)	18. (c)	19. (a)	20. (b)
21. (c)	22. (a)	23. (d)	24. (b)	25. (a)	26. (b)	27. (a)	28. (d)	29. (a)	30. (c)